Crucifixion

Ofsted Inspector

Angry Ex-Teacher

Disclaimer
Names have been changed to protect the identities of teachers, pupils and schools.
All events within are real; however, some have been merged with others for the purposes of this book.
No Ofsted inspectors were crucified during the writing of this book. Sorry.

Contents

Introduction

When I was a shiny new teacher full of ideals, I used to regard the longer-serving, more cynical occupants of the staffroom with something approaching detestation. Why had these people even gone into teaching when it was so obvious they hated dealing with kids? Why were they still here - two decades on - when they loathed the job so much?

Within a few years, I became one of those teachers. I saw new teachers coming in, so enthusiastic and malleable, and wondered how long each would last the course before either seeing the light and getting out while they still had some semblance of self-respect, or being destroyed and believing they really were as useless as politicians, the media, pupils, parents - and anyone who thought they could do the job better - kept telling them they were.

I became aware that new teachers were regarding me with the same loathing I used to feel for cynical teachers. In staff meetings, I wanted to grab those young whippersnappers by the lapels and yell that I used to believe too. That I fell into the trap of thinking I had to abide by all the petty rules and regulations to ensure I did the best for my pupils.

And isn't that what made us decide to enter the 'profession'? To do the best for our pupils?

Oh, how naïve we were!

We now have a state education system with underfunded schools; academy chain and free school managers raking in the dosh but getting rid of teachers' professional pay and conditions; a rising number of unqualified staff teaching all subjects; professionals who are ignored by those who know nothing of education; and a teaching profession on the brink of extinction. Not to mention the continuation of a largely irrelevant curriculum that cheats our young people out of the opportunity to acquire useful skills for life.

The past two decades have ensured that teaching is now more about arbitrary targets, data, tick boxes and league tables than anything close to educating future generations. Teachers and pupils - the central figures in any decent education process - are at the bottom of the list of priorities now adhered to by politicians and inspectors.

That's the system you'll read about here: the system that has been progressively destroyed to the point that those without a death wish are jumping ship. You will find a few genuine, dedicated, experienced professionals still clinging on, but these are in decline

It is mostly these people from whom I receive messages, opinions and anecdotes, many of which I share in this book. Some will make you laugh; others will make you spit; all, I hope, will make you reflect on the state of today's education system and appreciate what a wonderful job our teaching professionals do under very difficult – although sometimes hilarious – circumstances.

Whatever you take from this, I hope you enjoy most of it and that you will not be too offended by the language and some of my opinions. And please share your comments:

angryexteacher.wordpress.com
Twitter: @angryexteacher
Facebook: https://www.facebook.com/Angry-Ex-Teacher-1216442031721674/?fref=ts

This isn't what I trained for

'Aaron refused to clean his teeth so I told him you would do it for him,' declares Mrs Dogsthorpe, pushing her somewhat tubby son towards me whilst thrusting a plastic bag into my hand. 'It's all in there. Make sure he does the back ones properly.'

As I stare mutely after Mrs Dogsthorpe's retreating backside (Aaron obviously gets his genes from her – either that or they gorge together on lard butties whilst watching CBBC each evening) I remind myself that I have a BA Hons (2:1), a Masters and a Post Graduate Certificate in Education from one of the UK's most prestigious universities. At no time did it prepare me for this moment.

You would be forgiven, at this point, for imagining that I've wasted my degree by becoming a nursery or reception assistant – or a general helper in an infant-school at the very most - and that Aaron is a little cutie (albeit on the tubby side) wearing short trousers and clutching a book bag. But you would be wrong. I've wasted my degree by becoming a secondary school teacher - somewhere in East Anglia - and Aaron is a year 8 student in my tutor group, approaching his 13th birthday.

So, here I am, peering into a bag that contains a crusty, toothpaste-covered tube and a toothbrush featuring Ben 10 (but not many bristles) whilst a bemused Aaron gazes dumbly up at me. (I am not tall, but what Aaron has gained in width he has not gained in height.)

'So Aaron,' I say through gritted teeth whilst gingerly holding out the offending bag. 'Am I really going to have to humiliate you by cleaning your teeth for you in the staff toilets, or are you going to toddle off and do them yourself?'

He gives me what he believes is a menacing look, snorts, then snatches the bag from me before making his way towards the boys' bogs.

Just wait until I accidentally mention this in front of the rest of the form …

*

There is a serious point to this anecdote, though …

The idea that teachers are surrogate parents seems to have taken root over the last decade or so. Hardly a week goes by without the media reporting that some do-gooder is calling for teachers to teach kids the kind of stuff you'd expect them to have learned at home: what not to eat, how to use cutlery, how to sit on a chair, saying please and thank you, or how to wipe their arses and wash their hands when they've been for a dump. Are parents even needed these days?

I've seen an increasing number of children over the years who are unable to wait their turn to speak; who, even at secondary age, will throw a tantrum when they're not picked to answer a question; who are incapable of making sure they bring even a pencil with them to class; and who do not understand that their actions have an impact on others (although, even if they did understand, they probably wouldn't give a shit).

I know from colleagues working with four- and five-year-olds that an increasing number of parents are happy to leave

4

toilet training to their children's teachers. A recent visit to some parenting websites was most enlightening: although the majority of parents argue that teachers should not be expected to toilet train children, a higher than expected proportion argued that they should.

Bring on the BA (Hons) in Changing Shitty Clothes.

A typical start to my working day

My classroom is bloody freezing. This must be the coldest September on record, but there's no way the school heating will go on before the October half term. And to add to my bad mood, the room is still set up for the previous evening's governors' meeting, which means I have to waste precious time putting the desks and chairs back in their proper places.

As usual, I arrived at school at 7:30 this morning. After making two trips to my car to bring in the marking I'd taken home (I was kicked out early last night because of the governors' meeting that simply had to take place in my classroom) and sorting out Aaron's toileting, I was then collared by the pastoral care administrator, who wanted to discuss a particular year 10 student I have the misfortune to teach.

'Why have you given Dwayne Bates a detention for tonight?'

'Because he's an annoying little scrote.'

(Actually, I didn't use those exact words, but ten minutes after the conversation I had one of those 'Oh, if only I'd said….' moments.)

I then spent the next fifteen minutes trying to convince the pastoral care administrator that as Master Bates (I think this moniker is appropriate, as well as hilarious) had (once again) told me to 'fuck off and die' when I explained (once again) that he shouldn't throw plastic bottles full of water at other students, this did constitute a lack of respect as well as a danger to others and that, yes, the least he deserved was a detention.

No, I wasn't aware that the mutant's inbred mother was claiming that I pick on him at every opportunity. And no, I didn't call him a thick twat and say that I hated having him in my class. (Although I suppose it's possible, in my old age, that I have started unwittingly uttering my thoughts out loud.)

The admin bod soon buggered off when I told her in no uncertain terms that I would not be withdrawing the detention, and to tell Master Bates that I'd double the detention if he went snivelling to her again with tales.

Muttering to myself about fluffy, namby-pamby do-gooders - who don't have a bloody clue about teaching and just want to be best mates with the kids - I plug in my lap top and power it up so I can sort out the classroom furniture whilst the lap top takes its usual fifteen minutes to move from one screen to another. I notice that one of the display boards has had a corner liberated from the edging paper. Bugger. The head and governors will now feel the need to bring to my attention the fact that my classroom is looking tatty and unprofessional.

It is now 8:15 and so far I have achieved bugger all. Then the classroom door opens and Rachel, the head of student welfare - who, incidentally, isn't a teacher and doesn't have lessons to prepare - pops her annoying, grinning head round the door. 'Hiya!' she chirps. 'Just letting you know we're having an important child welfare meeting for all form tutors in five minutes. My room!' Then she's gone.

7

I clench my fists, shout 'Fuck!' and kick a chair across the room. I need to get this room sorted, get everything up and running on my laptop, check staff emails in case there are any other last-minute, allegedly urgent, events taking place today that I simply have to avoid, as well as set up for my four morning lessons. (I'm on break duty today so won't even get a chance for a piss until at least half past one.)

Five minutes later, the room is straight and the display paper patched up, but the laptop is still thinking about loading up. There's nothing else for it – I'll have to abandon it for the meeting, let my tutor group run riot while I set up for lessons, and hope the head doesn't walk in.

*

Of course, during tutor time, the head walks in.

'One or two governors commented on the state of your classroom last night, Mr Angry.'

A paper aeroplane skims past her right ear. 'Why are these young people not engaged in something creative and educational?'

I want to reply that making aeroplanes that actually fly is quite an achievement for Darren Dingle, but bite my tongue. 'Sorry – it's been a hectic morning. I have given them some word-searches with an alcohol avoidance theme' (this week's whole-school citizenship topic is substance abuse, and every teacher of every subject is expected to get it into their lesson plans) 'but … well … as you can see… they've been used for… and now I need to set up for my lessons…' I trail off as she begins nosing through the pile of exercise books I brought in this morning. Surely she can't complain that I'm not giving quality feedback in my marking comments.

'These comments could be more positive,' she sniffs. 'You have used the word "however" in this comment. Look. "Well done, Kayleigh. You have used some excellent similes and metaphors to describe the setting; however, you need to remember the excellent work you did in your spellings of suffixes last year."'

I manage a suitably meek expression. 'I see,' I say in a serious voice, whilst imagining her tongue lolling out of her dribbling gob as my hands grip her round her scrawny throat. 'I should have rephrased that to "Perhaps you could have improved this by applying the spelling rules for adding suffixes as you learned to apply them so well last year" rather than making the comment seem negative.'

She arches an eyebrow at me for a couple of seconds. 'If you know how to word comments positively, why don't you apply this in your marking?'

'I do most of the time, but I'm human and I get tired and there are only so many hours in a day and I missed my son's cricket presentation so I could get all the marking done with what I thought were helpful comments rather than a blithe 'well done' or just a tick, and I gave my wife an excuse for not snuggling down to watch *Silent Witness* because I had so much planning to do, and yet here I am on the back foot again and all you can do is criticise my display board, and where's my positive feedback, bitch?'

But, of course, I don't think of saying any of that until she's left the room.

The students in my tutor group are an interesting bunch. Our school, which from this moment will be referred to as Hell-on-High, runs what is called 'vertical tutoring'. This means that each tutor group has a mixture of all year groups within it. The premise for this is to encourage older students to mentor younger ones, and for younger students to feel less intimidated by the bigger kids. I think it actually works in some schools, too. At Hell-on-High, though, it just means that the younger kids are introduced to drugs and porn at a much earlier age – especially when their form tutor is too shagged out to organise 'creative and educational' activities and leaves them to fend for themselves.

I make eye contact with each student as I call their name for the register: it is not unheard of for students to answer on behalf of someone who's too busy having a fag or fingering one of the year ten girls round the back of the PE block.

'Chardonnay.'
'Yes Sir.'
'Kylie.'
''ere Sir'
'Marcin'

No reply. Marcin is Polish and, despite having lived in Britain for seven years, uses his nationality as an excuse to refuse to engage at any level with any teacher. I look round the room and see him sniggering over a magazine with Darren. I'm not even going to investigate.

'Angel.'
'Yep.'

A misnomer if ever there was one. Angel is in year nine and wants to be a pop singer. The fact that her singing voice sounds like Joe Pasquale after inhaling helium and that she looks like Frank Bruno after a good thrashing hasn't dampened her determination one jot. She would be better suited as a bouncer at the local gansta hangout. She scares the shit out of me, anyway.

'Darren.'
'Yeah, Sir. Hey Sir, you ought to see this!'
'No thank you.' I look back down at the register. 'Aaron.'
'Yo, dude!'
'Hey, Aaron dude, you have toothpaste round your mouth.'
(Ha! That shut him up, the little toe rag!)
'Siobhan.'
'Yes Sir!'

Siobhan is such a lovely girl. I wish they were all like her. It's not even as if she has a good grounding, as I realised when I met her mum the previous summer at the new year seven pupils' induction evening.

'Siobhan has good reports from all her primary teachers so I'm looking forward to welcoming her into our form ...'

I stopped suddenly when I noticed that the mother had turned a shade of purple. 'You bloody teachers are hopeless,' she growled. 'I'm Siobhan Frost's mother.' Mrs Frost pronounced Siobhan's name phonetically, so it came out 'si-oh-bhan''. Poor Si-oh-bhan looked mortified, bless her.

Some of the names parents in this area give their offspring are just criminal. I mean, as if it isn't bad enough having chav parents, they get saddled with stupid names such as 'Phoenix' and 'Hercules' and 'Princess'. It's even more cruel when Hercules, year nine, is smaller than the average year five child, and Princess is a slapper.

I once read on a renowned teachers' forum that there are students out there named 'Lucifer', 'Stella Artois' and even one poor girl called 'Chlamydia'! I really hope for the sake of the kids that these stories are untrue.

Then again, we teachers have to get our jollies where we can.

Some background (WARNING: contains Gove)

Years of being told how to do our job by government ministers, who know nothing of teaching, and for whom the post of Education Secretary is merely a stepping stone to greater cabinet posts, has completely eroded so many teachers' beliefs in state education and the good it can do. Each education secretary feels the need to put his or her stamp of authority onto education, pontificating about standards and the importance of 'education, education, education'. Yet not one seems to have considered the repercussions of their evidence-free initiatives: the wreckage of kids' education and wellbeing, as well as the almost complete annihilation of a whole profession.

I left teaching in 2012, while Gove (AKA 'Pob', 'Gargoyle' or 'That Clueless Arrogant Ugly Gobshite') was education secretary. He was forcing his archaic ideas of what education should be onto an already beleaguered teaching profession, ignoring evidence-based advice from many, many educational experts.

Just one example of this was his insistence on 'rigorous' (he used this word a lot, did Gove) grammar teaching. Bewildered primary school pupils (and their equally bewildered teachers, many of whom had received no grammar teaching in their own school days) were suddenly expected to be able to parse sentences, identify prepositional phrases, and spot the use of the passive voice when, for many pupils, just writing a sentence was a struggle.

13

Even renowned linguists bemoaned what children were being forced to learn as so much of it was absolute bollocks.

Meanwhile, secondary pupils were having a pretty shitty time as well. Exam boards were under instructions to raise their grade boundaries - *after* that cohort of year 11 pupils had taken their exams. Those who sat their GCSEs in June 2012 were told that they had not made the grade towards which they had been working. If they had been earmarked for a C, they were lucky to be awarded a D. Many were awarded E grades for the same level of work that, just the previous January, had earned their more fortunate early-entry year 11 peers a grade C.

Many school leavers in England that year were faced with no college place, no place in sixth form to study A Level, and no future to speak of. The Scottish government acknowledged the injustice of this and reviewed the marks, but English politicians didn't see the point.

Indeed, this cohort of young people, born between 1st September 1995 and 31st August 1996, were handed the worst deal of all. They were the first to sit the 'new and improved' GCSEs, in which coursework had been replaced by **controlled assessments**. Yet their performance was directly compared with that of school leavers in previous years who'd had the advantage of coursework that could be completed over time and at home.

Four years later, no lessons had been learned - well, not by politicians, anyway. Despite the work, training and cost that went into implementing this GCSE exam format, 2016 saw the end of the controlled assessment format, and many GCSEs from then on became 100% written end-of-year exams only. At the time of writing, we have just had the first cohort of school leavers awarded English and maths GCSEs whereby grades are levelled 1 to 9, rather than A* to G. And no one - not students, parents, employers, teachers or even the government stooges - seems to have a fucking Scooby how those scores compare with the previous grade boundaries.

There are many problems here: the cost to schools; the waste of hard work and time of teachers; and the inconsistency, irrelevance and poor quality of education - not to mention the confusion for employers and the potential impact on Britain's future workforce.

In this modern world, coursework makes so much more sense than a 100% expectation of timed, handwritten exams. The research, drafting and editing skills required for coursework are closer to that needed in the types of job that require good use of English, yet we are seeing a move back to the system from the beginning of the 20th century.

Then there's the inconsistency between the qualifications of young people only a few years apart in age. How many employers in 2018 will know that, out of the applicants for the same job, the sixteen-year-old with the equivalent to a C in GCSE English (it's arguable as to whether this is a 4 or 5 under the current system) has probably worked an awful lot harder than the 18-year old with a B, who in turn is likely to have worked harder than the 22-year-old with an A? And just to confuse things, there will be 22-year-olds with grade Cs who did their exams in January 2012 but who are worse at English than others who were awarded grades D or E later that year.

All in the name of 'rigour' and 'raising standards'.

Yes, standards did need to rise, and I was amongst those teachers who had seen the slide into mediocrity and campaigned to improve standards. That's not to say that all pupils who did well during previous years were mediocre: many were exceptional, but their only means of displaying many of their talents lay outside the school curriculum. As an exam marker, I'd been instructed to give high marks to A level English language students who seemed incapable of structuring coherent sentences - a problem that many of my employer acquaintances discovered. Many were employing those who, on paper, looked as if they were star language experts but who, when it came to basic grammar, punctuation and spelling, turned out to be below the ability of a grade C O-Level school leaver from 1984.

The way in which Gove chose to raise those standards, though, left much to be desired. He showed a breathtaking level of arrogance and a blatant lack of regard for the work pupils and teachers had undertaken. He introduced an even narrower curriculum that gave precedence to English and maths, almost to the exclusion of IT, history, geography, music, art, DT, PE, sports - even science. He assured us all that teaching was the problem, not the cash-strapped and resource-deprived state of schools. And he did it all with the backing of fellow politicians, the media and the general public.

At no time has there been an education secretary so hated by the teaching profession. He termed us 'enemies of promise' when we warned him that the curriculum was too narrow. He called us 'the blob' when we disagreed with his latest un-researched, mad-cap schemes. He portrayed us as greedy and unprofessional when we objected to the scrapping of our pay and conditions. Even those outside teaching were beginning to make ripples, especially parents. Not a vote winner.

In the summer of 2014, Gove was removed from education and given a low profile post. It's my belief that the Tories needed him to be forgotten by the general public by the time the 2015 General Election came round. His successor, Nicky Morgan, merely continued his legacy until she was pushed out after giving her support to Gove's PM bid following the EU Referendum in June 2016. The only positive thing to come out of that whole Brexit debacle was that both were relegated to the back benches, but Pob remained waiting in the wings, rubbing his hands and awaiting his moment. That came soon enough and he is currently Secretary of State for Environment, Food and Rural Affairs. We're fucked.

At the time of writing this, our current education secretary, Justine Greening, seems under the impression that she has made 'an historic reform' by announcing an extra £1.3bn funding for schools; however, this is nowhere near enough to cover the cuts suffered over the past few years, and has merely been recycled from other areas of the education budget.

That's a bit like taking away a kid's birthday presents, rewrapping them and giving them back at Christmas.

The following link conveys some of the problems:

http://www.independent.co.uk/news/uk/politics/school-funding-england-fall-5-per-cent-by-2019-ifs-fiscal-studies-education-justine-greening-a7846381.html

I had higher hopes when Greening first took the post. Sensibly, she announced the scrapping of her predecessors' plan to make eleven-year-olds retake their fit-for-nothing key stage 2 tests (SATs) in secondary school if they hadn't achieved what Gove considered to be a good level. She also seems reluctant to progress with the grammar school agenda. It will be interesting to look back on her legacy in another couple of years.

Almost a quarter of teachers who trained since 2011 had quit by 2016, mainly as a result of the pay cap and erosion of terms and conditions, as well as intolerable work load and no work-life balance.

This link highlights some of the reasons:

http://www.independent.co.uk/news/education/education-news/who-is-justine-greening-education-secretary-tory-conservative-election-2017-cabinet-theresa-may-a7786296.html

But instead of investing in the retention of the few excellent teachers still clinging on, the government would rather spend money on misleading adverts to encourage fresh young meat to the profession: people too young and naive to recognise how they are being manipulated.

STOP PRESS: Greening has just been replaced by Damian Hinds. Apparently Greening wasn't enough like Gove for May's liking. Watch this space.

Where's the respect and trust?

According to a recent poll, most people have great respect for teachers.

Here's a link – just in case, like me, you think this is an April Fool joke.

https://www.tes.com/news/school-news/breaking-news/most-people-have-a-great-deal-respect-teachers-poll-shows

You could have fooled me – and the majority of teachers.

I have noticed a significant rise in the number of parents who will come into school or telephone especially to assure the teacher that 'my child never lies'. So I must have imagined watching Ryan Baggot nudge his mates before sticking out his leg and tripping up a younger girl, then howling with laughter as the poor child scrambled around to pick up the contents of her bag. I must also have imagined him shouting, 'That's twenty points for a Pakki!' as I came over to see if the girl was OK.

Over the years, I have been accused of some unbelievable crimes against kids who, as far as their parents are concerned, are little angels, but who I'm sure are hiding the numbers 666 beneath their stupid haircuts.

What the fuck has happened to parents? When I was at school, I would hope that my parents wouldn't find out about my misdemeanours, otherwise I'd be in trouble twice over. These days, it seems, many parents see teachers as the enemy and imagine that the sun shines from their kids' arses.

To share all the examples of this behaviour I've experienced, as well as all those that have been sent to me by other teachers, would need a separate book. The next chapter outlines just one account that will convince you, if you are in any doubt, that kids have the power to destroy a teacher's unblemished career.

Mrs Jones and the false allegation

Mrs Jones was an excellent English teacher who had been at our school for twenty-two years. She was enthusiastic about her subject and was able to instil a love of poetry and literature in the most reluctant students. Just the kind of teacher every school wants.

However, as is the case with many effective teachers, there were students and parents who did not appreciate her adherence to the principles of hard work and respectful behaviour, so they chose to make her job as difficult as they could.

The extent of their hatred became apparent at 8.30 one Tuesday morning, as Mrs Jones was preparing for the teaching day. The deputy head teacher marched into the classroom and demanded that Mrs Jones make her way immediately to the head's office, taking her personal belongings with her.

An allegation had been made against her to the effect that she had hit a year ten student round the head the previous day. The allegation had been backed up by another student in the class, and Mrs Jones was to be suspended forthwith, pending an investigation.

She was sent home and told she was not to contact other members of staff. We were not aware of this until just before the first lesson, when the head of department told us that Mrs Jones would not be in for the foreseeable future and that we were not to contact her.

21

Of course, the first thing most of us did was to send supportive texts and ask about her wellbeing. All teachers know that they are at the mercy of kids who 'know their rights' but for whom responsibility is an unknown concept, and once we'd heard what had happened (gossip from the kids) we knew without doubt that the story was fabricated. There was no way Mrs Jones would have hit a student.

That evening, I visited Mrs Jones with a bunch of flowers and a bottle of wine. (Luckily the weather was icy so I was able to disguise myself with a woolly hat pulled over my head and a scarf covering most of my face – just in case the British Gas van parked across from the Jones's house was one of the head teacher's lackeys.)

Mr Jones let me in. I was taken aback when I saw his wife sitting in an armchair, red-eyed and shrunken. We talked for a long time and it transpired that she had not been informed as to the identity of the student who had made the allegation, but had a fairly good idea who it was (and was professional enough not to share her suspicions with me). There had been a teaching assistant in the room at the time of the alleged incident and Mrs Jones had asked the head teacher to get a statement from her. Whether this had been done yet, no one knew – we were not even sure that the teaching assistant knew of the allegation. Yet the student making the allegation was at liberty to mix with classmates and ensure everyone had their stories synchronised.

I sought out the teaching assistant the following day. She had indeed heard about the accusation: not officially from school managers, but from gossip among students with whom she had been working. Mrs Jones' plight was, by now, common knowledge throughout the school and the community.

This teaching assistant went straight to the head teacher and asked for her side of the story to be acknowledged. She was sent off to write a statement about what had happened in the classroom on that day.

What happened next restored my faith in young people. The head teacher was presented with a letter, signed by some of the students from the class where the incident was alleged to have taken place, attesting that the allegation was completely false. The boy in question and several of his mates had told members of the class what would happen to them if they did not back the allegation, and had been heard bragging that they were 'teaching that Jones bitch a lesson'.

But still the 'investigation' continued, and by now everyone knew who the accuser was.

Other teachers refused to have this boy and his friend in lessons but were overruled because, as the mothers of both insisted (along with the pastoral care team and their ilk) their sons had every right to their education.

This horrible situation continued for more than a week, with Mrs Jones none the wiser as to the definite identity of her accuser – only what 'gossip' she could pick up from others - and with teachers tip-toeing around the accusers and other potential trouble-makers, who were starting to realise that they were on to a sure winner when it came to intimidation of their teachers.

Fortunately for Mrs Jones, she belonged to a union and was able to get support from them. An initial meeting was organised between her, the school managers and governors, to which she brought a union representative.

Within half an hour the whole case had been thrown out as inadmissible and the school managers given a good bollocking by the union rep for not following procedures correctly. They had failed to get witness statements as soon as they knew of the allegation; they had not given the teacher a chance to defend herself; and they had allowed the accuser, as well as his friends and parents, to blow the whole fictitious episode out of all proportion.

For Mrs Jones, the experience was one she could never forget. Following the meeting, she handed in her resignation and took the rest of the term off sick, vowing to never again work in a school.

That was 2011, and she has stuck to her guns. But what a sad loss to education. And how much worse things could have been if, as is the case with many teachers, she had not been a member of a teaching union.

But what of the fate of the accuser? Well, he stayed at the school and continued to disrupt lessons for his peers – as was his 'right'. And there was bugger all any teacher or decent pupil could do to prevent this.

Pupil behaviour

During the 1980s, and quite rightly, in my opinion, corporal punishment was abolished in British state schools. The threat of the cane, a constant threat during my own school years, was finally at an end.

Since then, however, standards of behaviour have plummeted, as have teachers' authority to deal with this.

School children have always denigrated their teachers amongst their peers. This is a form of entertainment as old as education itself, and something all teachers learn to live with. Unlike today, though, such comments were never shared with parents, and certainly not with the teachers at whom such comments were aimed.

Many pupils today have no hesitation verbally, and sometimes physically, abusing their teachers, often with the backing of their parents.

During my time as a teacher, I have been called: bastard; fat bastard; fat cunt; fat twat; fat old twat; old fucker; grumpy fucker; thick fucker; fat fucker; ... . (No doubt you have noticed a 'fat' theme developing here: I have a slow metabolism.)

Some schools are worse than others, but overall I am expected to accept this as part and parcel of being a teacher. I can't refuse to have a pupil in my class just because he told me to fuck off when I asked him to stop shouting at me while I was speaking to the class.

I have also had many objects thrown at me. Full water bottles. Heavy text books. Chairs. Desks. Other pupils. Again, I am obliged to continue welcoming the perpetrators into my classroom.

Sometimes when I speak to parents about such behaviour – and a few times when I've mentioned this to mates down the pub – I've been told 'Teachers should expect that sort of thing' or 'If you can't deal with kids, you shouldn't be a teacher'. Even school managers – many of whom have forgotten what it's like to actually work with kids in a classroom – will plead for a kid's right to disrupt lessons rather than the rights of classmates and teachers to work in a safe environment.

If you told your GP to fuck off, or called him/ her a cunt, or threw an object at him/ her, what do you think would happen? What if you did that to the receptionist? Or a shop assistant? Or your boss?

You'd be barred from the surgery/ shop/ place of work, which is why this sort of thing doesn't happen very often in those places. Teachers, on the other hand, are fair game. We should 'suck it up' as part of working with young people.

What sort of lessons are we teaching kids with this attitude? That it's OK to verbally or physically abuse someone who is trying to help you?

I hear from employers how they find it difficult to train and keep some young employees, many of whom seem to think the world owes them a living. They have been taught that they can be as foul as they please in order to get their own way and that someone in authority will bail them out. Many are shocked to realise that the adult world doesn't work like this – or at least not until they have sprogs of their own and can go back to terrorising teachers.

Punishments

When I was at school in the olden days, pupils got away with very little. Although not a particularly naughty kid at primary school, I was on several occasions smacked hard by my teachers. The only crime I remember committing to earn this humiliating punishment was pouring water into the sand pit, which was situated in the cloakroom just outside our classroom. I was six. I'd been on several beach trips with my family and knew that the best way to make sand castles was to add water. Surely that was why there was a sink situated a few paces from the sand pit?

I went home with a very red leg, which I had to hide from my mum in case I got a matching hand mark on the other.

Others from my generation were subjected to 'the slipper': a device the teacher kept in her/his desk for the express purpose of smacking little kids on the backside. Some thought it amusing to chalk a sad face on the sole of said slipper, so the poor kids who had been caught running in the corridor/ scribbling in the corner of their book/ pissing in the sink because the toilets were overflowing would be further humiliated by having to wander the school with that telling chalk face on their arses. And then getting a clip round the ear at home when mum had to wash the offending skirt/ pair of shorts.

Secondary school wasn't much better, but by then punishments had become a badge of honour amongst the more 'lively' pupils, as well as less likely to actually prevent the behaviour that earned such punishments. The cane was the punishment of choice in many cases: a trip to the headteacher's office whereby one would hold out their hand, palm up, and be subjected to the number of whacks appropriate for the crime. At my school, swearing was worth one, but blaspheming (it was a church school) was worth two. Truanting lessons was worth three, and setting off the fire alarm when there wasn't a fire was worth four.

Don't ask me how I know all that.

Sauntering into a lesson following a caning was seen as heroic and rarely prevented repeat behaviour. Detention, however, was another thing entirely. Detentions meant having to cancel after school arrangements: sports matches, liaisons on the school bus, the latest episode of Grange Hill - all were forfeited. Detentions were most often handed out to those who had not completed homework, or who were not deemed to have worked hard enough during lessons.

Getting detention was not cool. And there was no way out of it. If you didn't turn up, your detention time doubled, so you were better off just attending. Most parents would support the school with detentions - probably because they got an hour's extra peace from the little scrote bags whilst someone else dealt with them.

There was no letter home with a minimum of 24 hours' notice so that little Scroty could make arrangements for mumsy to collect him. Yes, he'd miss the bus. Yes, it would be dark. And yes, there was a chance that someone might want to mug him on the way home for his school-approved black, leather brief case. But there was no chance for Angry Parent to march into the school to assert their child's rights. (Not that they ever would. Well, not mine, anyway.)

No. You pissed about during period five, you stayed behind that evening. No arguments. No discussions. Your crime, you paid. And chances were you'd make damned sure you didn't have to do detention again.

Now, detentions are more of a punishment for teachers than the kids. To my mind, detentions should be boring for pupils - or at least some form of torture - but now teachers are expected to provide unpaid private tuition to the toe rags who prevented the rest of the class from accessing that day's education. And it's not unknown for Chavvy Parent to march into school during little Scroty's detention, demanding their right to take him home.

Even expulsion is no longer a valid threat as kids and their parents know they have all the rights without any of the responsibility, and schools are now failed by Ofsted for excluding too many kids.

What's the answer, then? There's been talk of getting military-trained staff into schools to improve discipline, but that shouldn't be necessary. Politicians and the media could take the first, important step by acknowledging teachers as professionals and giving them the praise and respect they deserve. Too many parents are merely reacting to the media's demonisation of teaching professionals and are passing down their contempt to their kids.

For those kids who persist in being shit-bags: exclusion - whereby parents are 100% responsible for said shit-bag's behaviour - would be an effective deterrent.

But that's not a vote winner, so is unlikely to happen any time soon.

30

Often, pupils can be so disruptive that teachers pray they won't turn up to their lessons.

This account from Amy, a secondary teacher, also sums up how intimidating such pupils can be.

Zamen and Lloyd were two huge year 11s in my bottom set English class. Thankfully, they rarely turned up for lessons, but when they did it was always for maximum disruption. One particular Friday, period five, they turned up fifteen minutes before the end of school bell, demanding I sign their report cards. Both had been warned that, unless they received ticks for every point for which they were on report that week, they would not be allowed to the Y11 prom.

I told them they would have to wait until the bell had gone before I could even look at their reports cards. The inevitable fuss followed: I was called all the names you can imagine and the lesson for the rest of the class, difficult enough last thing on a Friday, was destroyed.

Both boys knew that other teachers would sign the cards just to get rid of them, and I was tempted to do so for the sake of the other kids in the class and the upcoming GCSEs, but I was heartily sick of the pair of them behaving like gangsters, knowing they had us all in the palms of their hands.

By the time the bell went and I'd dismissed the rest of the class, both boys were right in my face, calling me a bitch and telling me what I shit teacher I was.

I looked down at the points on Lloyd's card:

31

1. *Arrive to lessons on time with equipment*
2. *Allow the teacher to deliver the lesson without unnecessary interruption*
3. *Complete the work set*
4. *Show respect and consideration for your classmates*
5. *Show respect to your teacher.*

I put a cross beside each point.

Lloyd was indignant, to say the least, and stormed out of my classroom, kicking desks and chairs as he went, shouting that he would get me sacked, and slamming the door so hard the room shook.

Then I turned to Zamen. He glared at me challengingly, but I did the same to his card.

'Why did you do this?' he screamed in my face.

'Show me one of those points that you have fulfilled,' I replied, trying not to show how scared I was. It was just the two of us in the classroom, with a bunch of his jeering mates waiting outside.

'When did I show you disrespect, you bitch?' he yelled.

He put his hand out as if to shove me, but I stepped back. Through gritted teeth, I hissed, 'Fuck off out of my classroom.'

As soon as the words were out, I regretted them, but the look on his face was worth whatever trouble might follow. He stared at me for a few seconds, mouth agape, then flung open the door and yelled, 'Miss X just told me to fuck off!'

'Oh yeah,' jeered one of his mates.

'Fuck off, Zamen!' shouted another.

He glared at me. 'I'll get you sacked for this!' was his parting shot.

I worried all weekend that I would lose my job, and quite frankly I wasn't too sure how bothered I was, but nothing more was ever said, and Zamen came to no more of my lessons. It would seem that no one believed him.

I was gutted, though, to learn that he and Lloyd were allowed to the prom after all.

Really, who can blame kids for behaving like this if they know they're going to get away with it? One can only hope that, some time soon, they'll piss off the wrong person and have the shit beaten out of them.

When naughty kids are funny

I have to be honest, though - there have been times when kids behaving like - well, kids - would have me howling with laughter, often to the disgust of my colleagues.

A loud fart in Y10 assembly once had me and half the staff rushing into the corridor so the hysterical kids (and the stern headteacher who'd just asked for that last comment to be repeated as he didn't quite catch it) wouldn't see our tears of laughter. A photocopy of a sketch from the back of an artistically talented year 11's English exercise book, depicting

33

one of the assistant head teachers with a penis for a head, adorned the staff room notice board for several days before the aforementioned dickhead spotted it and tore it down. A Y9's shocked face when he realised I'd seen him running behind the head teacher in the dinner hall, jerking his fist and mouthing 'wanker'. (Astute kid.)

I think one of the funniest was the day I returned following a training course, during which a supply teacher had covered my lessons. I experienced a stint of supply myself for a few weeks and it's not something I'd recommend to any teacher. Kids' cruelty can be relentless and supply teachers are fair game. I don't approve of supply-teacher-baiting and always leave very firm instructions for pupils and TAs about my expectations.

On this occasion, however, one of the attendance administrators greeted me with a frown and a sheet of paper the kids of one year 10 class had had to sign as a register because the official copy couldn't be found (the gits had hidden it).

This register, which the supply teacher had unwittingly handed in to the attendance office, included the following names:

Adolf Hitler
Suck My Cock
Steve Jobs (who had recently died)
Richard Head
Dick Wad
Micky Mouse's left testicle (although this had been spelled 'testicul')
Back Sack'n'crack
Lennie Small (we were studying Of Mice and Men, so I was particularly pleased with this one)

Simon Cowell's Trousers

Gove Isacunt (this kid will go far!)

Cameron Isacunt (I knew who this was: he always copied someone else's work)

Shakespeare Sucks

Romeo was a kiddie fiddler ...

I was laughing so much I could read no further. As the attendance administrator droned on about how this was a waste of her precious time and that my Y10s were a bunch of yobs, I was planning how I would use these names as I called that day's register.

You've just gotta love kids sometimes!

'They Who Shall Not Be Named'

The following has been adapted from one of my blog posts:

I need to whisper this just in case any teachers are listening: ..."*Ofsted.*"

My favourite Ofsted joke:
What's the difference between a cosmetic surgeon and an Ofsted inspector?

A cosmetic surgeon tucks up your features, but an Ofsted inspector ...

Seriously though, an impending Ofsted visit is enough to put the fear of god into the most stalwart teacher. The lengths that some schools will go to in order to get that much-coveted 'good' grade would be amusing if it were not so tragic, and would provide enough material for a separate book of its own. What I will share with you here are just a couple of my experiences that show how Ofsted changes its goalposts to keep teachers twitching for months after they have left the building.

First, at the risk of sounding smug, I have to mention that, at the time of the incidents described here, I had been watched by five inspectors at three different schools, and every judgement had been 'outstanding'. Yet this did not fill me with confidence. I knew that the whole Ofsted rigmarole was a game and that I had merely been lucky to have been watched by fair inspectors whilst I worked with reasonable classes. I knew that a truly good or outstanding teacher needed to produce much more than the items on an Ofsted inspection list, and that these needed to be produced at every lesson, not just when performing for Ofsted.

Anyway, things for me were about to change.

I was working with a bottom set English class, and as with many bottom sets it contained a few difficult characters. As well as those students who had recently settled from Poland, Lithuania, Portugal and various places around the African continent, there were those who had made the choice simply not to engage in lessons.

Of course, this was the only lesson of mine that day honoured with a visit from an inspector. She sidled into the room, wearing a grin that could have been worn by the Grim Reaper after the Great Plague.

I'd just managed to get the class settled and now they were fired up again. Grim Reaper did not seem perturbed by the curiosity of the less socially aware in the class: 'Ooos that?' 'Woss she doin' 'ere?' 'Is you 'ere to watch sir? 'e's crap!'

I indicated a vacant seat next to Mandy Wagstaff, the girl I suspected hadn't been near a bath or shower in the past twelve months. I then attempted to calm the class again, and psyched myself up for the inevitable carnage.

The students had been given a quick starter activity to complete in pairs and had started on that. As with all things for students of this level, the resources were designed to be visually appealing and fun in order to have any chance of engaging their interest.

37

During a normal lesson, all the students, no matter how sullen and disengaged, would have joined in with this. But of course this was not a normal lesson. There was a new audience to impress, with the added knowledge that teachers live in fear of Ofsted.

Let the fun commence.

'Siiiiiir! Luke just chucked some paper at me 'ead!'
'No I didn't you fuckin' liar!'

Without stopping what I was saying, I walked over to Kylie's desk and picked up the ball of paper then wrote both names on the board, as per the school's behaviour policy. (Normally I wouldn't have bothered, but this was a performance, after all.) Luke was not pleased.

'Oi, you fat bastard. I told you I didn't throw it! Why have I got a warning? You're always pick...'
'Luke, you swore and that gets you a warning. I'll come and speak to you about it in a while.'

At this, Luke stood up, kicked his chair across the room and stomped towards the door where he stopped and glared at the inspector. Pointing at me, he shouted, 'I 'ope you sack this fuckin' cunt. He picks on us all the time!'

To the sound of applause and banging on desks from others in the class, Luke made his exit, slamming the door for good measure.

Quickly, I gave the students a two-minute activity linked to the lesson so that I could, as per school policy, send an email to the key stage 4 leader (again, not a teacher) informing her of Luke's departure. I felt the need to conduct a commentary of my actions to the inspector, conscious that this was further disrupting the lesson. I could see her scribbling away, much to the delight of certain members of the class.

Eventually I was able to get the students working at the activities I'd planned for the main part of the lesson. As all the students were strugglers, there seemed little point in assigning myself to work with a particular group: I knew from experience that would mean little or no work from the others, so I walked around the classroom during the activity, giving prompts to students as and when I got to them.

Again, had this been a normal lesson, most of the students would have had a go and there would have been three or four waiting to be prompted at every step. I made a point of visiting the real strugglers first, but while I was trying to translate the instructions for our latest Polish student, something kicked off at the other side of the classroom, so I went over there quickly to sort it out.

Ryan had drawn a rather deformed-looking penis on Charys's book, so she had retaliated with what looked to me like a cauliflower but, as Charys informed me delightedly, 'It's me nan's minge, sir!'

And so the lesson continued thus. And while this was going on, the inspector was 'interviewing' students about their targets and progress and what they enjoyed/ didn't enjoy about English lessons. This was the most animated some of them had been since they'd started school: perhaps the first time they had really felt what it was like to have some kind of power.

"Targets? What are they? Sir didn't tell me nuffink about no targets. He's a shit teacher."

I flicked to the inside covers of each book and instructed the pupils to explain to the inspector how they had to fill in their target boxes on a regular basis. Most swore they had never set eyes on these boxes, despite the fact they had obviously spent hours scrawling Manga characters - and more deformed willies than you'd find at a clap clinic – all over the sheet.

I'm sure you don't need me to tell you, dear reader, that this lesson was not graded outstanding. The amount of work I'd invested in preparing that lesson wasn't even considered. The differentiation I'd employed to allow for barriers such as language/ emotional turmoil/ not possessing a brain were not acknowledged. All the inspector could say was that I should have worked with a small group and left the others to work independently.

I tried to explain that my decision not to do so with this particular class was based on past experience, where often I finished up with lots of work from the group but nothing at all from the rest of the class other than pages full of deformed genitalia – some on the display boards as well.

She also commented that I hadn't included any **mini plenaries** throughout the lesson. Again, I attempted to explain that, due to the amount this group manages to take in throughout a whole lesson, any mini plenaries would in fact have been microscopic plenaries, but this carried no weight.

The behaviour of certain members of the class, she informed me, was because the level of activity was inappropriate for this group. She could not elaborate, however, on whether it should have been more or less challenging and was unprepared to believe that in a normal lesson the level would have been just right. I'd been teaching this group since September so I knew them a lot better than she did. But this cut no ice with her either.

Just to add insult, the following day I was observed with the same group (Luke lasted five minutes longer than he had the previous day) by a different inspector (a man this time) who informed me that I was wrong to work with a small group and should have walked around the classroom helping students as and when they needed it. Oh yes, the behaviour was my fault because the lesson was not appropriate. He could not, however, give me any actual advice as to how this could have been more 'appropriate' and even had the temerity to say,' You're their teacher so you know them better than I'.

Quite!

From that day, I vowed to teach how I saw fit, and bugger the advice from those who did not have to teach my classes. The pass rate at the end of the year was my best ever – and the best in the whole department. According to Ofsted, though, I was a less-than-satisfactory teacher.

So, one more Ofsted joke:
Q   How many Ofsted inspectors does it take to change a light bulb?

A   Six. One to change it; one to read the plan on how to change it; one to observe the changing; one to write it up; one to assess; and one who doesn't seem to have a purpose, but it makes for an even number.

More Ofsted (and where you find out where the title for this book comes from)

Dan - a year four teacher - had worked hard with pupils to write, direct and cast the Easter production for the church junior school in which he worked.

This was an important annual event at the school, and one that parents looked forward to, as well as something that met the Ofsted criteria for religious study in church schools.

It seemed all the hard work would be wasted, though, when Ofsted inspectors called the school to announce they would be visiting the following week - the week leading up to the Easter holiday - right slap bang in the middle of the performance week.

The head teacher called an emergency staff meeting in which he told his staff that the production would be called off so the school could focus on the points Ofsted would want to see.

Dan was more than a little upset. Apart from all the hard work he and the pupils had put into the production, and the disappointment children and parents would endure, this was a church school and it was approaching the most important celebration in the Christian calendar: the crucifixion and resurrection of Jesus Christ.

Now, I'm not a religious person, but I do think that any parent who sends their child to a church school is entitled to expect that school to mark important Christian occasions. And I also expect Ofsted to understand that.

But so great is the fear from head teachers for their jobs that they will allow a complete overhaul of their daily - often excellent - procedures in order to put on a show. And Ofsted inspectors know this goes on.

Dan tried to argue this with the head. The production would showcase the literacy skills of the pupils who had written the script; the costume design that took place in DT lessons; the artwork for the scenery; the excellent listening skills and behaviour of those taking part; and the teamwork required for older pupils to help younger ones with learning lines and scene changes.

But the head was having none of it. Ofsted wanted to see proper lessons in proper classroom settings, against which they could tick their pre-prepared boxes, crunch numbers and create graphs to show school performance.

What Ofsted did see were classes of disgruntled pupils who felt their hard work was worthless, and parents only too happy to tick the 'unsatisfied' boxes in the parent questionnaire.

When it was announced that the Easter play would take place *after* the Easter holiday, by which time the actor playing Jesus would have moved to his new school, one pupil asked, 'Sir, can we crucify an Ofsted inspector instead?'

Teaching is no longer a profession

Can you imagine doctors being told that when they apply for posts they will need to be interviewed by potential patients? And that these patients have no medical knowledge whatsoever?

Let's go a bit further: what if they had to be interviewed by their child patients? Young people who are considered too young to work or have a vote, but who are being told that they have an important say in the future career of someone who is professionally trained in their occupation?

What about if police officers were interviewed by members of the community they would serve – including some of the children and the well-known trouble makers? How many would agree this was a good idea?

Teachers have studied for their 'profession' for at least four years, yet it is deemed perfectly acceptable for them to be subjected to a pupil interview panel. This happens in primary and in secondary, with children of all ages, academic ability and standards of behaviour/ misbehaviour.

When I was at school, there were teachers we liked and respected, but there were many more – good at their jobs – whom we hated with a passion. And any opportunity to get one over on them was considered fair.

As acknowledged earlier, pupil and teacher conflict is as old as education. It's expected and, to some degree, accepted.

What has changed, however, is the manner in which teachers are now perceived and treated. When I was at school and wanted to be spiteful about a teacher who had given me a detention, I would wait until I was with my mates, sharing a fag behind the bike sheds and muttering malicious fantasies about the demise of said teacher. Never, though, would I have made those feelings known to that teacher – or, in fact, to any other adult. I knew there was a line to be drawn; we all knew what was and was not acceptable behaviour.

Today, however, pupils' rudeness and disrespect to teachers is quite shocking and at a level that would not be tolerated in any other field of employment.

Not a day goes by without at least one student telling me I'm a stupid bastard or to fuck off and die. All I am trying to do is my job – to teach these kids something that will one day be useful to them. Because they are children with relatively little experience of the world, they often don't grasp the importance of what I am attempting to do for them. It is therefore important that children understand that teachers have expertise and that they deserve respect. But if the adults making the rules don't acknowledge that, what hope is there?

If I had thought for one minute that I could have got away with it, I would have been openly rude to some of my teachers. If I had known that there would be no follow up to my foulness; that society protected me from being expelled from school; that my parents would blame my shortcomings on my teachers; that the government and school managers would castigate teachers no matter how hard they tried to work; that Ofsted inspectors and school managers would see my inappropriate behaviour as a failing of the teacher rather than my own choice, and that the teacher would be the one to receive the sanctions....

What would you have done at the age of sixteen? Or eleven? Or five?

But as if that is not bad enough, children are given the perception of their own increased power by being told that they can interview teachers; that they have the power to decide on a professional's career. There's even a three-day training course for them. Four years for an adult to qualify as a teacher, but three days for a child to be able to make decisions about how good those teachers are.

I know more than one teacher who has stood in front of an unruly class, being informed that 'you only got this job because we like your jokes/ sweets/ tits'.

The school managers who allow this shocking disrespect towards teachers will argue that they use only the 'good' pupils. There are still issues with this, though, as even the good kids are just that: kids.

And what defines a 'good kid'? Do the senior managers of a school actually know the kids' personalities?

Quite a few schools use the chance to be on a teacher interview panel as a bribe for some of the 'less good' kids, and this had been widely reported in the press and on teacher forums.

Here are two links to one such report:
http://news.bbc.co.uk/1/hi/education/8599485.stm
https://www.theguardian.com/education/2010/apr/03/childre n-job-interviews-questions

We now have the concept of 'student voice', which doesn't help. I remember being elected by my classmates to represent our form on the school council. I was very excited: this was around the time Grange Hill was first on our screens, and the kids on that programme were able to debate the banning of school uniform. Nothing so exciting in real life, I soon discovered. I had a say in which charities to collect for, and was expected to help organise events for these. I also helped to organise a tuck shop which made a small profit for the school, as well as attempting to come up with solutions to bullying.

The thing that I was never allowed to forget, however, was that the teachers' voices mattered more than ours: they were the ones with professional training; they were the ones who knew what to do; they were the ones we and our parents respected.

I'm not arguing that this is how it should be: God knows there were more than a few sadistic and poorly trained teachers around then. But there must be some middle ground between that and the shambles we have today.

As many teachers have learned over the past few years, 'student voice' is taken so much more seriously than 'teacher voice'. Indeed, the student voice agenda is a misnomer: it should be 'arsehole voice' as arseholes seem to be taken far more seriously than other students. In fact, the 'student who actually wants to get on and learn without constant disruption from arsehole voice' agenda is criminally neglected.

Students have a voice, as do parents, but teachers – the professionals – the ones who have been trained to teach – have no voice at all.

But we're professionals when it suits

Teachers have to put up with a lot of bile from those who have no idea how hard they work, and one of the most common accusations is that we are not 'real' professionals.

I remember one parent in particular yelling at the new, young teacher in the classroom beside mine. The teacher had, quite reasonably, asked the parents to come in and see the state of the brand new textbook their little gobshite had destroyed and asked for the parents to pay to replace it. The mother responsible for spawning aforesaid gobshite was having none of it, yelling, 'I ain't paying out for no crappy book! How dare you speak down to me! You're a public servant and I pay your wages!'

As I explained to the new teacher (who was all for visiting the supermarket at which this particular mother was a shelf stacker so she could knock down the bog roll display) sometimes you just have to bite your tongue and suck it up: there's no arguing with fuckwits.

But occasionally - just occasionally - you get the chance for revenge. We had to wait a few months to get this woman back, but that day arrived.

It was the following January, one dark, freezing evening as I was entering yet more pointless data into the school system instead of getting through the pile of mock GCSE marking that

49

was threatening to topple into the bin, when the mother of Gobshite rapped on my classroom door and sidled in, trying to smile but managing to look like Michael Gove drinking his own piss.

'Sorry to interrupt you, Mr Angry, but I'm taking Gobshite on holiday and he ain't got no passport.' She placed a form on my desk, along with two photos of her son looking as if someone had shoved a cactus up his arse. Handy for future mugshots, I remember thinking. 'We need a professional to sign the form but the doc ses we 'ave to pay.'

Now, I had done this favour many times for other parents and friends, particularly those who respect my professional capacity, but I wasn't going to make it easy for this creature.

'What does your GP charge for doing this?' I asked, sliding the form towards me, resisting the urge to gob on her son's photograph.

'Thirty quid!'

'Really?' I replied. 'That's pretty cheap. Your GP must really like you.'

'Cheap?' she replied. 'To put a signature on a bit of paper? Bloody daylight robbery, if you ask me. That's why I'm asking you to do it. It sez 'ere teachers are professionals.'

I sucked loudly on my teeth – the way car mechanics do when they're about to shaft me for repairs on my battered Audi – and arranged my face into a sympathetic expression.

'But there's so much more to this than merely placing a signature on a form, Mrs Gobshite's Mum,' I said solemnly. 'I have to put my professional reputation on the line in the hope that you are not giving any false information on this form. I have to spend time reading through it, checking details, checking photos and dates. I can't possibly do it here and now.' I smiled reassuringly at her. 'Do you see my dilemma, Mrs Gobshite's Mum? Being a professional comes with lots of responsibilities.'

I could see her mouth working, but no words were coming out; just a strange guttural sound. Eventually she managed 'Can I have it tomorrow morning, then?'

'Of course,' I replied. 'Once I've finished this pile of marking,' I indicated the tower of mock GCSE papers, 'cooked and eaten my dinner and said hello to my wife and kids, I'll attend to Gobshite's passport form. Shall we meet here at, say, 7.45 am tomorrow?'

She looked taken aback. 'I don't want to get here that early. My shift doesn't start until nine- thirty tomorrow. Can't I come at ten-to-nine when I drop Gobshite off?'

'Ah, no.' I sighed, shaking may head and manoeuvring my face into what I hoped she'd think was a regretful expression. 'I'm afraid my professional work schedule won't allow that. How about this sort of time, then?'

She agreed to come back the following day after school. I waited until I was sure she was off the premises, then did a tour of the school, seeking out every teacher I knew taught Gobshite.

The following evening, I eagerly awaited the visit. She was bang on time, which was a first for her.

'Ah, hello,' I beamed. 'Sit down, sit down.' I picked up my laptop bag and produced the still unsigned forms.

'Now then,' I said, picking up my pen and clicking it ready for action. 'Before we start, will you be paying by cash or cheque?'

'What?'

'The £20 fee for my professional signature.'

Her mouth opened and closed for a couple of seconds. 'You're going to charge me?'

'Well, I spent an hour reading through your details, checking them against the school records, not to mention taking time from my busy schedule to sign the forms and photographs for you now,' I said. 'Normally I charge £30, but as I get on so well with your son ...'

She snatched the forms, dropping the photos of her gurning son on the floor. 'I'll get someone else to do it!' she spat, picking up the photos and marching out of the classroom.

I waited about twenty minutes for her to return, remembering how my colleagues had taken no persuading yesterday when I'd asked them to quote £30 for signing passport photos. 'OK,' she muttered through gritted teeth as she shuffled back into my classroom. 'I'll have to use a cheque.'

'Lovely,' I replied with a gracious smile. 'Just make that out to Hell-on-High Academy School Fund, would you? We need to replace some text books.'

The de-professionalisation of teachers

In most professions, age and experience bring respect and kudos. It is recognised that those who have been doing the job for a long time understand the pitfalls and are in the perfect position to hand down their acquired skills and knowledge to those with less experience.

This is no longer the case in teaching. Currently, many experienced teachers are treated with contempt by their managers and by less experienced staff. They are portrayed as cynical, self-interested and no longer 'up to the job'.

It is true that there are teachers still in classrooms merely because they need to see out their time until retirement, but this is not entirely down to being incapable of doing the job: it is mostly down to not being allowed to do the job the way they know it should be done.

Teaching is tiring. Even young entrants to the profession will at some time experience that bone-numbing exhaustion that overcomes one without warning, especially towards the end of a long term. Many new teachers are aghast to find that they are ill at the beginning of every school holiday as their bodies finally stop producing the adrenaline needed to get through a busy term. For some teachers, this is something that lasts all through their careers.

As teachers become physically and emotionally better able to deal with the demands of teaching, however, they discover how little their skills and knowledge are appreciated by those who run education. Those who have been teaching for more than a decade – and particularly those approaching retirement - are seeing old schemes and educational concepts coming round again – perhaps more than once – and can see them for what they are: old ideas given new labels and presented as the latest great solution to educational problems.

It is immensely tiring and frustrating for teachers to change the way they do their jobs several times a year, at the whim of the latest education secretary. Then a couple of years later there is a new education secretary, so the 'old ways' are debunked. The longer a teacher has been teaching, the more tired and disillusioned they will become. And the more likely it is they will see recycled schemes coming through with new labels.

This is one of the reasons that, in recent years, there has been an increase in the number of younger and less-experienced teachers being promoted to senior management positions within schools. These teachers are still reasonably fresh and, unlike their more experienced colleagues, haven't 'seen it all'. Therefore, they are more likely to run with every new initiative that the latest education secretary introduces, without realising that it will not work. They will expect their more experienced (but now subordinate) colleagues to run with these schemes, and will see any sign of resistance as evidence that these teachers are no longer up to the job.

There is an increasing number of older and more experienced teachers being held to account for disagreeing with the rapid changes occurring in education today. These hard-working, dedicated and genuinely caring professionals are being portrayed as lazy and reluctant to move with the times: as Michael Gove labelled them, 'the blob'. Their cynicism is seen as something that drags down the quality of education, when in fact it is the rapidity with which changes are implemented without valid research and evidence that is the true obstacle to good, honest educational success.

With all the government cuts in the public sector, it is even more apparent that older teachers will take the flak. Over the years, they have earned their stripes and their perks. They are paid a higher salary as is accorded experienced teachers. They will have a reasonably good pension (which they have well and truly earned) when they reach the age of sixty. By the time they retire, they won't have paid as much into the pension fund as new entrants to the profession, yet they will get their money sooner - and they will get more of it. In short, as far as this government is concerned, older and more experienced teachers are a financial liability. And furthermore, they know too much.

Most of these teachers still hold those ideals they had at the beginning of their careers, but now accept that they will not be the ones to make those ideals happen. If they raise their voices they are vilified, so keep quiet and knuckle down as best they can, keeping a low profile and hoping not to be sacked for incompetence.

They are disillusioned, scared … and bloody knackered.

Corrupt head teachers

If you follow my blog posts, you will have read an account of my experiences with a corrupt headteacher who had no scruples when it came to getting rid of excellent teachers, just because those teachers thought for themselves and would question any initiative that didn't have a direct positive influence on the pupils they taught.

I receive many messages from teachers and former teachers who have been used by head teachers to spy on their colleagues, or have been on the receiving end of a self-serving head on a mission.

Here, I share just a few of those many accounts.

Karen entered the teaching profession as a mature trainee, following a successful eleven year career in publishing.

I came into teaching by accident. I was taking time out to be with my two small children and started getting involved with kids' clubs and organisations. I realised very quickly that I was good at relating to children and looked into a career in primary teaching.

I got my first teaching job in 2003 and for the first two years I felt as if I'd found my true vocation in life. Of course there were downsides about the job – every job has those – but for the most part I felt fulfilled and useful; I felt that what I was doing really mattered and made a positive difference to the lives of real people.

I worked far more hours than I had in my previous career and was getting paid a lot less, especially when I worked out how many hours a week I was really putting in, but felt it was worth it. I took a lot of stick from friends about 'short days' and 'long holidays' but it didn't take long for those closest to me to realise that the reality was very different. But still, I really enjoyed my new career and no amount of time spent creating lessons and resources felt like hard work.

The rot didn't begin to set in until 2005, when I was given the post of Literacy Co-ordinator at a new school and placed on the school leadership team.

I saw my role as one of support for staff, as well as being the person ensuring that literacy teaching throughout the school was effective. I would happily spend the non-contact time allocated to me to help those members of staff for whom English language and literature didn't come naturally (the same as the Maths Co-ordinator had to support me with maths sometimes!) but it became apparent very quickly that the head teacher viewed her leadership team as spies: there to oversee her agenda and catch other teachers out.

At first I found myself being summoned to the head's office and told to 'pop in' to certain teachers' lessons (it was always the same two teachers, both of whom had been at the school a number of years) at particular times, but without forewarning. She would give me a list of negative points to look out for, which I was expected to report back to her.

This type of observation by stealth was, I knew, against all the accepted tenets of teaching, and certainly contravened union guidelines. Also, I had a lot of respect for the two teachers concerned. Both were in their late forties and had seen a lot of initiatives come and go over the years: they knew what would work and what would not and were, quite rightly, scathing about some of the initiatives that our head teacher was quick to adopt in an attempt to impress the LEA.

As I was unhappy with the arrangements, I took it upon myself to forewarn the affected members of staff prior to my visits, explaining what it was the head teacher wanted me to find. One teacher played along at first for the sake of the visits, before realising that his pupils were losing out and going back to his usual (excellent) teaching style. The other refused point blank to play the game and, right from the start, continued putting the needs of her pupils first.

When reporting back to the head teacher, I was at pains to explain how well the pupils in each class were doing on a regular basis, citing examples from their books and their obvious knowledge when they talked to me about their lessons. The head did not want to hear this: she wanted evidence that she could use with the governors to get rid of these teachers, simply because these experienced people did not always agree with everything she decreed.

Within a few weeks, both teachers were put through capability proceedings, despite all the good work they had done – and were still doing – with their classes.

I remember trying to get advice from other school managers on a teaching forum, but it quickly became apparent that I was in the minority when it came to seeing older, more experienced teachers as caring professionals. Almost all respondents were teachers who had been teaching a short time and who saw their swift elevation as evidence of their own brilliance rather than realising they were probably being manipulated.

59

My conscience could not deal with being part of a system that treated its experienced staff in such an unfair way, so I resigned and did some supply teaching.

Over the years, several head teachers have expressed an interest in employing me as a permanent teacher, encouraging me to apply for posts in their schools, but having seen from a management point-of-view how teaching has the potential to be so corrupt, I could never go back to it. I'm not as financially well-off as I was, but my conscience is clear and I can sleep at night.

Karen sent this account to me a year ago, while I was collecting material for this book. Today, she has left teaching completely and has returned to a post within publishing.

As she said:
'I went into teaching to make a difference, but found that I was allowed less and less to actually teach. I figured that my contribution to education was negligible so I may as well do something more rewarding for me and my family. I do miss teaching, though, and know I was bloody good at it.'

The following was sent to me by Paul, a young entrant to the teaching profession who rose rapidly through the ranks.
Within the first week of my NQT year I knew I'd made the biggest mistake of my life. I'd been ignored, laughed at and sworn at more than I'd ever been in my life and that was just from other members of staff. Everyone was so stressed and support for new teachers was zilch.

There was a new head teacher who had been brought in to raise standards. Other teachers said he had never actually taught. I don't know if that was true but he really didn't seem to know anything about the real challenges in a classroom. Anyway, he was a nightmare and always looking for people to blame. It was clear he was trying to get rid of some of the more experienced teachers. I was one of many NQTs; we didn't have a clue what we were supposed to be doing, and there weren't enough experienced staff to help us. The few who were there were permanently stressed. The atmosphere was horrendous.

Somehow I got through the first two terms without having a breakdown but I was one of the lucky ones. Other NQTs who started with me did not do as well: two were on long-term sick leave, one was suspended because of a pupil allegation (which was false but took some time to be sorted out) and one just walked out of her classroom one morning and never came back.

Just before the Easter holiday of my first year, I was asked to be the acting deputy head of the maths department as the deputy was going on maternity leave and her replacement had gone off sick with stress and depression following a run-in with the head.

I was delighted: it was more work but also more pay and I thought that I was being recognized for being a great teacher. I found out later that others with far more experience had already been asked and had refused to take the post because of the bullying behavior from the head teacher. I was a last resort.

That final term of my first year was awful. The crappy pay rise didn't make up for the amount of time I had to spend

61

sorting out departmental issues, as well as the number of meetings I was expected to attend and collect data for. And to top it all, the department head walked out following a disagreement with the head teacher and I was made department head to begin the following September. The amount of work I needed to do over the so-called holiday was unbelievable.

All through the summer holiday, I was getting emails from the head teacher demanding detailed plans for the department for the following year and requests to discuss certain 'lazy' members of staff he wanted me to lean on hard.

I managed to get a week of holiday before having to go in for A level and GCSE results, and by the time the summer bank holiday came round I was into autumn term mode.

That was four years ago, when I was 23. To look at me now you'd think I was at least 45. I'm shagged out!

I am now an assistant principal, in charge of some who mentored me and warned me to walk away while I still had a life. Many of my friends and family talk of my meteoric rise in the teaching profession, but I know it's bollocks. I just happen to be the mug who said he'd do it when no one else would.

I have no life. I don't often get to spend time with my girlfriend or my mates and when I do I'm just really stressed out about how much work I have to get done. I'm expected to oversee a system that I don't believe works for most students. I'm a complete fraud but I'm too proud to give it all up just yet. I'm approaching 30 and looking at more than 30 years more of this shitty existence with this shitty salary and a shitty pension at the end of it which I probably won't get because I'll be dead by the time I'm 40.

What I really hate about the job though is how I'm expected to treat professionals who know more about teaching than I could ever hope to learn - people who have chosen to work in teaching to make a difference. Many of these people are far more qualified than I am to run a school. They all know how to teach their subjects yet they are treated like shit from those above. I hate being a part of that system.

Ordinary teachers are targeted too

One morning, Sarah's head teacher informed her that she would be expected to take her year six class on a week-long residential trip following their **SATs.**

Now, a couple of years before, Sarah had taken this same class, when they were year fours, on a three-night trip to an activity resort. There had been many problems, the main one being no sleep. For three nights. Yet she and the two TAs who'd accompanied her were expected to be alert and take full responsibility for these little cherubs every minute of every day they were *in loco parentis.*

Despite rules about no phones, no sweets and a limited amount of spending money, many of the little darlings had been packed off with goodies, instructions to call and text several times a day, and to spend money every time they saw a shop.

Parents thought the rules were stupid and that this teacher, who was giving up her own time for no extra pay but lots of stressful responsibility, was just trying to spoil the kiddies' fun.

63

During the first day of activities, Sarah had to deal with: sobbing kids with broken phones; sobbing kids who had lost money; sobbing kids regurgitating Haribos; phones ringing; kids falling off equipment whilst chatting to mummy; mummy demanding to speak to 'that stupid teacher of yours' who wasn't keeping an eye on her little soldier; one mum who wanted to speak to Sarah, demanding to know why she wouldn't let Ryan eat the crisps and chocolate she had provided for him to share at breakfast; and kids who really did not know how to behave, and who constantly told their teacher 'You're not my mum!' when she tried to get them to hand in their phones/ sweets/ money for her to look after.

Not one parent thanked Sarah or her helpers when they came to pick up their children on the Wednesday evening (many of them late as they were at the pub/ had been watching something on telly/ couldn't be arsed). And the following day – understandably knackered, as were the kids - Sarah was expected to deal with parents who wanted to complain about how their sons' and daughters' trip had been ruined by her insistence that they couldn't share the peanuts Darren had brought in case Sophie suffered an anaphylactic shock.

Sarah vowed that never again would she take kids away, as did the TAs who had been with her. After all, how many jobs out there expect you to parent others' kids 24/7 with no extra pay or thanks of any kind, where the arse would be sued off you if a child was hurt or taken ill because kids and their parents didn't see why there should be rules?

But now here she was being told by the head teacher that she had no choice; she would be taking her year six class away for a week.

64

Sarah's own daughter would be in the middle of her GCSEs while the residential trip was taking place, so Sarah refused, as was her right.

Now, Sarah was an excellent teacher who worked more hours than any of her colleagues and who genuinely cared about the education of every child in her class. But she didn't see why it was an expectation that she should be mummy to them for a whole week. She and the head argued and eventually a member of **SLT** came to tell Sarah that she herself would be going, despite having to miss her own daughter's 5th birthday. As Sarah told her, that was her choice - she wasn't doing it.

Some weeks later, about a fortnight before the trip, that member of SLT announced she was pregnant, so would be unable to supervise the year six residential. Once again, Sarah was told she would have to do it. Once again, she refused.

The following day, that same member of SLT arrived in the middle of Sarah's literacy lesson 'just to observe some of the children'. A couple of days later, the same happened during a maths lesson.

A week later, Sarah was told to meet the head and the SLT member who had observed her, where she was presented with a list of targets to meet if she was to avoid **capability proceedings**. One of those targets was 'work as a member of a team' and the recommendation for meeting this target was to take her class on the residential trip the following week.

Sarah resigned the following day, asserting her right not to go on the trip (in the end, the head teacher had to supervise it) but had to work until Christmas as the deadline for summer resignations had passed.

As a result of the blatant bullying she received from then on, she was signed off sick in July and did not return to see out her resignation period. Because of the stress and anxiety she was under, she was in no fit state to look around for other posts and didn't feel that teaching was a profession in which she wished to remain.

She took on some supply work and was quickly snapped up by another school, but the whole experience left her angry and bitter. She realised soon that her new school was no better than the old one and she now firmly believes that all schools are the same. Even those with decent headteachers have the potential to be just as toxic as soon as a new head is appointed, or when once-decent heads are put under intolerable pressure.

Sarah now works for an IT company. She's bored but has lots of time to spend with her family and realises that she is actually better off - health-wise and financially - as pro-rata, she actually earns more per hour she has to work.

Yet another fantastic teacher lost.

Caring head teachers
are bullied into corruption

What about those head teachers who have managed to see through the government rhetoric and have clung on to their integrity?

Amongst the many messages I receive are quite a few from head teachers who have dared to put education before government initiatives.

Here I share just two.

Debbie started teaching in the mid-eighties and was a primary school head for fifteen years

I empathise with my staff and with my pupils and do my very best to ensure all are treated fairly to enable my school to be truly outstanding.

Unfortunately my ideals do not match those of Ofsted, the government or academy trust executives.

Our school became an academy just over a year ago, and is now run by a multi-academy trust. This trust manages quite a few schools and is under pressure to ensure certain targets are met, otherwise schools are removed from their authority.

One of the trust executives asked me last year to remove some of the year six children from the school data to help us reach the latest impossible target we'd been set for that year's test results. I refused to do this. I don't agree with the tests in their current form, and I also disagree with this obsession within education for league tables and data performance, and especially with having to cheat to achieve these false targets.

When the results came through, they were exactly as the teachers had predicted; however, and also as expected, they were below those expected by the trust.

Within a week of the results, I was told to go as the governors had reached a verdict of 'no confidence' in my leadership. (I since learned that this was not the case, but the trust gets what the trust wants.)

An interim head was put in place the following September, but by the first half term almost all the teachers had resigned to leave that Christmas. This did not please me as much as some might think: it is the children I worry about. It has always been the children. But the academy trust cares only about its targets.

Pat was a secondary head for almost twenty years:
Head teachers get a lot of flak from teachers in general because we are seen as too scared to stand up to the more stupid initiatives handed down to us, particularly when those initiatives are damaging for pupils. Yet when I stood up for my pupils and staff by refusing to knuckle under, no one fought the governors' decision to have me replaced.

Many of the pupils at my school struggled with academic subjects but excelled at more practical things, such as sports, design technology, drama or music. It seemed ridiculous to try to make a pupil who struggled to read study a Shakespeare play – a soul-destroying experience for the pupil and the teacher that just reinforced failings rather than highlighting true strengths and talents.

68

Despite edicts from above, I insisted that pupils at my school would not have to work towards impossible targets. Many of the year 11s had guaranteed posts in construction and related industries lined up for when they left school and were looking forward to a life of independence; there seemed no point torturing those who hated literature and saw no value in it with hours of analysing poetry.

I was prepared to get my staff to make sure these young people had a good standard of reading, writing and maths, as well as the ability to think for themselves and make good decisions. My own less-academic school friends had taken CSEs rather than O Levels and are now very happy with life, many of them more wealthy – and healthy - than I could ever hope to be.

My brave (some would call 'foolish') decision to put pupils first, although popular with parents, teachers and the pupils themselves, resulted in the end of my career.

Perhaps if more head teachers would refuse to be cowed by edicts from above, education would not be in the mess it's in now, but I don't think many will be taking that risk, no matter how much they believe they should.

Why are so many teachers suffering from stress-related illnesses?

If you've read this far, you won't need to ask this question.
The blog post that received the most reaction on my website was on this topic, so I have shamelessly copied it here.
If you'd like to see some of the comments, here's the link to the post.

https://angryexteacher.wordpress.com/2012/11/20/why-do-stress-related-illnesses-appear-to-be-increasing-among-teachers/#comments

Many people send messages requesting I don't share them in case they are identified, so obviously those will not appear. Some of those messages are simply heartbreaking – and I'm not usually an overly emotional person.

Why do stress-related illnesses appear to be increasing amongst teachers?
The number of teachers suffering from stress-related illnesses – particularly depression and anxiety – seems to be on the increase. Just a quick browse on the Health and Wellbeing and Personal fora of the **TES** discussion boards shows a disturbing rise in the number of teachers posting for advice on how to deal with the symptoms of severe anxiety and depression.

The majority of these posts suggest that such distressing symptoms are brought about by teachers' current working conditions and the pressures under which they find themselves.

Many of these posts start off the same. A poster is worried that they cannot keep on top of their workload, despite working long days and weekends. Added to this, so much of what they are expected to do doesn't seem to have any bearing on what is needed for their students to learn and progress. This is leading to pressure from management and causing teachers to feel that they are not working hard enough or are failing in some way.

A good deal of these posts come from long-standing posters with 'good' reputations (the sort who have been posting on the boards for years, who generously share resources and offer help and advice to other teachers). They post for help with symptoms which other posters recognise as depression or anxiety as they have suffered (or are suffering) themselves. They are advised to visit their GP. The poster avoids this as they 'don't have time' or think they should 'pull themselves together' and get on with it. Some will say that, despite being told to take time off by their GPs, they would feel more stressed if they weren't at work to see that everything gets done properly.

Most of these end up posting a couple of days or weeks later in a desperate state as they have broken down in tears at work and been sent home; they are now at a point where they cannot function normally.

The level of 'support' some of these posters say they are getting from their employers is shocking. Some are expected to email cover lessons every day they are off sick; some are inundated with phone calls from school asking when they are going to be back; some are even told by their bosses that they have been off too long and will be put on capability (where they are subjected to even more intense observations, criticism and expectations to justify their existence in the school).

The one thing that all these posters have in common is their obvious distress at being unable to do their jobs properly. The feeling that they are letting down their students and colleagues is obvious from their posts. They feel that they are being weak or are malingering because they are not running round like headless chickens. It is becoming more apparent among health professionals that depressive illnesses are often the preserve of the hard-working and conscientious. It is by no means an illness caused by weakness.

When such people are working in an environment where pressure and criticism are rife, they will do their utmost to meet expectations at all times. When these expectations grow, so too does the level of hard work and self-sacrifice from such people. Through all this, they have to endure the almost daily negative messages that come from politicians and the media, reinforcing the stereotype of the lazy, whingeing teacher. These already exhausted and anxious people redouble their efforts in an attempt to dispel these negative images.

Eventually, something has to give.

The effects of teacher illness, as all these affected teachers recognise, can have untold consequences for the students they teach. Some schools will be responsible and ensure that classes, particularly those with exams approaching, have a fully-qualified teacher standing in so pupil progress is not hampered any more than it could be otherwise. Many schools, however, do not. They will condemn the students to a long line of cover supervisors or TAs, or teachers who are not qualified to teach that subject. This knowledge causes even more stress for teachers who are ill and often results in their returning to the workplace too soon. They then become even more ill when they try to rebuild the bridges that fell due to their absence – but not through their fault.

It doesn't take a qualified psychiatrist to recognise that today's culture in teaching is a health bomb waiting to explode. Simply piling more initiatives, more pressure and more negative press on beleaguered teachers is not the way to ensure a good quality education for our young people (not to mention the stress that current targets cause pupils of all ages). If teachers are not treated properly, they will not be able to function at the high standards expected from them. Not for long, anyway.

New teachers go into the profession wanting to 'make a difference'. They feel privileged to work so closely with young people and to have the opportunity to help them learn, progress and grow into responsible adults. Sadly, for many, this passion is knocked out of them before they have served five years in the profession.

Many of the cases of depression now being seen are suffered by teachers who have been in the profession for a number of years and have proved in the past what it is to be an excellent teacher. Many of these are now seen as too expensive: they have earned their stripes and their perks but, if not in a managerial role, are considered to be unambitious or just plain rubbish.

Not every teacher wants a management role. Management roles take teachers away from the classroom. Management roles mean kowtowing to some of the ridiculous bureaucratic systems that good teachers know will make no difference to the quality of education. Some teachers want to do that for which they trained: teach. They don't want to play the game that successive education secretaries insist we play so they can con the public into believing the latest DfE mantras.

The types of initiative needed in schools today need to focus on ensuring that:

- Children get the best education
- Teachers are given the time, resources and support to deliver that education
- This education is appropriate for pupils' capabilities. There cannot be a 'one size fits all' education. All children are different and all progress at different rates. (Of course, this will also mean spending money on special schools and specially-staffed units within mainstream schools.)
- League tables and unrealistic targets are abolished
- Good teachers are rewarded accordingly (and this is not necessarily linked to results – but if the above are established then rewarding by results would indeed be fair)
- The public is able to respect teachers once again by not being bombarded with negative, unsubstantiated claims from politicians and media.
- Education is run by education professionals and not politicians

I often rant about how the current school system is increasing the stress levels in pupils as young as primary school age. The constant grind and 'points for improvement' are no good for anyone's self-esteem. There needs to be a time when students and teachers alike are told that they are doing a great job and that it is recognised that they are doing their best with the resources they have at their disposal. It needs to be recognised that not all children can succeed academically and that those who don't should not feel that they are worthless. Instead, they should have other options available to them to retain their self-esteem.

Education should be aimed at the pupils' needs and be something they enjoy as well as something that challenges them. Trying to put square pegs into round holes is stressful for everyone and this needs to be recognised.

Nowhere in this rant have I made suggestions for improving the duty of care school managers should have for their staff. I think it's fair to say that, with the above points established, teacher wellbeing would improve dramatically. And with that so too would educational standards.

If only improving education was the name of the political game.

Let's lighten the mood now

Here's one of my favourite anecdotes, which was sent in by Mandy, a former primary teacher (who left teaching at the age of 48).

During my first week at a new school, and while I was still getting to know the lively little characters in my year 4 class, I had to begin a PSHE (Physical, Social and Health Education) unit on body awareness. The first lesson required the class to come up with names for different private parts of the body. I knew this would be an awkward, giggly lesson and that the children would no doubt find the whole thing hilarious (as would any eight- or nine-year-old) but nothing prepared me for some of the things I heard that afternoon, and it is one of those lessons that I will remember for the rest of my life.

I decided that we would begin with synonyms and pet names for 'bottom' before moving on to male and female private parts. I mean – what's the worst a bunch of nine-year-olds can come up with?

Here's a selection of words I expected to hear:

- *Behind*
- *Backside*
- *Bum*
- *Buttocks*
- *Butt*
- *Arse*
- *Crack*
- *Ass and Fanny (we had an American in the class)*

76

Here are the words and phrases I did not expect to hear:

- *Black hole of Calcutta*
- *Dumpster*
- *The back door*
- *Turd cutter*
- *The captain's quarters*
- *Dirt box*
- *Fudge-packing factory*

For goodness sake - these kids were eight and nine! The lesson was an absolute scream. For them. I was shocked and, I admit, very amused; I learned a lot that afternoon, including lots of jokes about bums. Here's my favourite:

'Doctor! Doctor! I need a new arse. This one's got a crack in it!'

And no, I'm afraid we didn't ever move on to synonyms for genetalia: I just couldn't cope.

Why performance-related pay (PRP) won't work in education

This has been adapted from one of my blog posts

Some time ago, Hell-on-High Academy introduced performance-related pay (PRP) for its teachers. This budget could be distributed, based on annual appraisals and at the discretion of the head teacher and governors, among the teaching staff.

Within the existing staff, Hell-on-High has an English teacher, Mrs Smith, with thirty years' experience and an exemplary record. She is popular with parents and those students who want to do well in English; many parents request that their children are taught by her. Each year her students either reach or exceed the targets set for them.

Miss Green was a newly qualified teacher (NQT) last year and this will be her second year teaching at Hell-on-High. Because she is relatively inexperienced, she is given 'easier' classes: those with fewer trouble makers or serial under achievers. Whereas the difficult classes used to be shared between Mrs Smith and her recently retired colleague, Mrs Smith now has them all and, as a result, cannot have as many of the less-difficult classes. But she is a more experienced teacher, so this is fair.

Isn't it?

At the annual appraisal later in the year, it is noted that Mrs Smith's percentage of achievers has dropped considerably. This is no reflection of her skills as a teacher or the level of work she does: indeed, she has worked harder and longer this past year in an effort to get those students who don't value education – along with their parents – to engage. But, as the old saying goes: you can take a horse to water but you can't make it drink. (Or, as I prefer to say: it doesn't matter how much you polish a turd, it'll always be a turd.)

Mrs Smith will not receive her salary increment this year.

The school is paying full whack for the seven members of the senior management team (all of whom rarely teach). Also, the new, young head of the humanities department is paid a premium becuase of the high percentage of good exam results in geography and history. (It's worth bearing in mind that humanities subjects are optional after year 9, so the workload and risks of pupil disengagement with those subjects are considerably less.)

Other teachers, Miss Green among them, will receive their annual salary increment because they are lucky enough to have year 11 classes where the majority of students would have achieved good results whatever the circumstances, and because of the good foundations set for GCSE students by teachers such as Mrs Smith when those pupils were in year 9 and 10.

Meanwhile, Hell-on-High needs to recruit more teachers for the following school year.

The number of teachers receiving a salary increment is depleting the budget somewhat, so the head teacher and governors cannot afford to employ teachers deserving of the

79

higher pay scales. Despite advertising for outstanding teachers, they cannot afford to pay the outstanding teacher rate so will need to attract those who have a less-than-perfect record.

Even if Mrs Smith were to go for interviews at other schools, she will be judged on her latest annual appraisal. And if Miss Green goes for interviews at other schools, she will be perceived as a better teacher.

In the midst of this bureaucratic nightmare, what is happening to educational achievement? It may look on paper as if Miss Green is the better teacher, but who would you rather have teaching your child?

The thing is, parents: you will never know. Well, not until it's too late.

What should education be for, and how does PRP undermine that?

When education was first made compulsory, it was thought that all children, whatever their background, should have the same opportunities. OK, many personal circumstances played a big part in ensuring that the poorer children remained at the bottom of the pile, but as time went on the inequalities became less polarised. (I acknowledge that they didn't disappear completely, but that's a whole other discussion.)

Long ago, when Hell-on-High Academy was just called Hell-on-High School, it was one of several schools in the region that shared resources and ideas: in general, making sure that all students in the region had the same opportunities, whichever school they lived near.

80

Since the introduction of school targets and league tables, however, this no longer happens. Now, Leafy Suburb Free School no longer shares innovation and good practice with Hell-on-High because they can't risk the competition. Hell-on-High jealously guards its few successes for fear that Leafy Suburb Free School will push them off the 312th spot on the league table. God forbid they should give Ofsted an excuse to visit earlier than expected.

This has been going on for a few years and is one of the key contributors to a poorer quality of education in the town. But it's about to get worse.

Because of PRP, not only will school be pitted against school, but teacher against teacher within the same school. Even within the same department.

Neither Hell-on-High Academy nor Leafy Suburb Free School has the funds to pay all its teachers the top rates. Teachers at both schools are now looking after number one and are vying with others in their departments for the status of 'best teacher', and this is having an effect on the overall teaching standards in both schools.

54-year-old Mrs Thomas, Hell-on-High's longest serving maths teacher, having seen what happened to Mrs Smith from the English department, is now wary of sharing good practice with Mr White, the newly-qualified maths teacher she is supposed to be mentoring. She doesn't want to lose her annual salary increment, but helping him to teach well means that she might. Consequently, the pupils Mr White teaches are missing out on some excellent teaching methods.

Who wouldn't do the same as Mrs Thomas? Teaching has become a dog-eat-dog job. (I won't use the term 'profession' because we all know that teachers are no longer accorded that respect.)

I repeat: no school will have the funds to pay all its teachers top rates. Does this mean that they will knowingly employ teachers who they know are less than outstanding? Or will genuinely outstanding teachers be forced to work for less?

The idea of education as an equal opportunity for all is, in England, quickly becoming a thing of the past.

And that leads me to tuition fees ...
Remember reading about the good old days, when only the rich were able to access a good education, thereby ensuring they kept their place amongst the wealthy in society?
Then some pesky socialists decided that was unfair, and before we knew what had hit us, plebs from all walks of life were given the opportunity to be educated and enjoy some of the finer things in life.

Well, fear ye not: the good old days are returning.

Some years ago, grants were abolished for the majority of young people wanting to access higher education and replaced by student loans. The logic behind this was that university graduates would enjoy a lifetime of higher earnings, and that it was only fair that, once earning such vast salaries, they should pay back into the state that which they had taken out.

For some, this was a fair resolution. But for many – some of whom were conned into believing their degree in leisure and tourism would make their fortune and who now earn minimum wage on a zero hours contract – it means a lifetime of paying for something vastly overpriced and unfit for purpose.

This is much worse now since the introduction of tuition fees, and particularly since universities can now charge in excess of £9,000 per year for higher education.

Yes, there is help for the very poorest of society, but there are far too many obstacles along the way for many to benefit, so for the majority higher education can be no more than an unobtainable dream.

If you come from one of the few very rich families, however, you don't need to worry. You could be as thick as shit but enjoy a superior education to your more intellectual but much poorer peers. And you'll never have to share a lecture hall with a smelly pleb.

Hip! Hip! Hurrah!

Gove's legacy

Sorry, but it's impossible to have a really good rant about the current state of education without referring to him.

When the education system should be doing more to suit the future our young people are heading towards, Gove has ensured that we remain firmly rooted in the past for a good few years yet.

Just take a look at the changes he made to the exam system. First, the abolition of coursework for GCSE subjects such as English. Yes, there were problems with this, as in some pupils merely copied essays from the internet and passed them off as their own. So because of a few stupid kids, the majority of hard-working ones have to suffer – as do those who will employ them in the future.

We live in a world where the majority of jobs – indeed, the bulk of life outside work – necessitates at least a basic grasp of computers. There probably are some very specialised jobs where employees need to be able to reel off a three-page, hand-written essay in the space of 45 minutes, with no opportunity to edit, cut and paste until it's to one's liking, but I'm struggling to think of one.

The majority of people in our schools today who go on to use their writing skills - in employment and in general life - will do so with the benefit of word software of some description.

Furthermore, those who go on to A Levels and university will need research skills: the ability to know where to look for relevant information, be able to discern the best quality primary and secondary resources, and be able to reference their sources. All the skills that were introduced within English coursework, but which now have been removed.

Thanks to Gove, we are returning to the system introduced many decades ago – before computers were in general use. If you doubt that, look in any school exam hall during May and June. Rows of kids sitting in silence, scribbling away about something they've never even considered before opening the paper, and having a set amount of time in which to complete an essay on it. By hand.

The world has changed. The skills needed to work in today's world are very different from those required 20 years ago, yet the system is heading back to at least the 1950s.

We need to move forward with education, and that means having those who understand the purposes of education running the show: not backward-looking politicians who base success on arbitrary targets and league tables.

English literature is another casualty of Gove's legacy
When I first started teaching English, I was quite dismissive of the importance of literature: for me, language was the be-all-and-end-all.

Over the years, however, my opinion has changed entirely. (Although the jury is still out with poetry and Shakespeare: do kids who struggle to read any text at all really benefit from being forced to analyse ancient or flowery language?) I have witnessed even the most immature and shallow year 10 and 11 pupils become quite philosophical when confronted by some of the themes encountered in literature; very often, this is the first opportunity some kids have to think critically about the real world. And isn't that a huge part of what education should be about?

Some of the most interesting discussions and critical essays have come from pupils' reading and understanding of themes within such texts as *Of Mice and Men*, *To Kill a Mockingbird* and *A View From the Bridge*. Concepts such as racism, inequality and justice - all important issues in the real world.

'Justice isn't always fair, is it?'

'Sometimes you have to break the law to make things morally right, don't you, sir?'

'Why did it seem to be ok then to treat people differently because of their colour/ gender/ age?'

'Did the writer know there was a problem with racism/ ageism/ sexism/ elitism when they were writing this? Is that why they wrote it or did they think it was just normal to treat others like that?'

All the texts I mention above have one thing in common: they are no longer on the curriculum for GCSE English, simply because they were not written by English writers. Guess whose bright idea that was.

Yes, there are plenty of English texts that cover important themes of interest to kids:

'Why isn't it ok for thirteen-year-olds to marry now?'

'So, was Romeo a paedo?'

86

... but I've yet to find one that covers the above themes in such a real and engaging manner. Generations of kids have enjoyed these texts, and very often can talk about them with parents who remember studying them in their own school days.

The British are inward-looking enough without dismissing the work and thoughts of other English-speaking nations.

Education is a political issue

But should it be? Granted, compulsory education for the masses began as a political initiative and without that we'd be in a much worse state than we are today.

Having said that, the extent to which central government became involved initially was minimal. This did mean that we had pockets of Britain where educational standards were much worse than others, and it's clear to see that so much historical involvement from education secretaries has been well meaning, even if often unhelpful.

Today, the central micro-management of education is most definitely having a negative effect, not just on teachers but on pupils and parents too.

I've written many times about the fact that Nick Gibb, our schools minister who has decided upon the nature of the Spelling, Punctuation and Grammar tests (SPaG) for primary school children has no real understanding of how language works, assigning narrow rules that even some of the most pedantic grammarians would ignore, and certainly argued against by those far more qualified than he on the subject. Yet, despite the evidence (and his own public cock up when presented with some of the same questionable rules he expects children to abide by: https://www.tes.com/news/school-news/breaking-news/listen-schools-minister-trips-grammar-question) he is determined to press on with his evidence-free SPaG agenda.

Successive education secretaries have been determined to put their own stamp on education policy, with the result that today's schools are struggling to recruit and retain teachers.

Contrary to right-wing tabloid rhetoric, teachers are not in the job for short days, long holidays and gold-plated pensions. The majority just want to be able to bloody teach without endless initiatives from those who know bugger all about what the job involves.

As with the NHS, education is being taken down the privatisation route. One sure way to convince the public that a service needs to be privatised is to deprive it of resources then, when it inevitably collapses, tell the public it is time to rescue it. Cue PM's cronies investing money to 'rescue' that service. And we know that very few people who are good at making lots of money will invest in something that won't generate even more for themselves.

Already we are seeing founders of free schools and academies being charged with using school funds for extravagant director perks, whilst the schools they manage struggle to recruit teachers or buy educational resources. We have also seen so-called 'super heads' giving up after a short time in post - even their inflated salaries are not enough to persuade them that this is a battle they can win.

We can be grateful that, unlike many countries, we have had past governments that insisted that education is a right, but now, instead of moving forwards, we are going back to an educational golden age that exists only in Gove's head.

Even the arts are given less prestige than they were a century ago. Nicky Morgan warned students against taking arts subjects as they would, apparently, earn less money. (Try telling that to successful writers, actors and musicians). And arts are being squeezed out of the curriculum for even our youngest children in favour of maths and English grammar.

As for sports ... well ... just compare Britain with Australia. And those Brits who have been successful at sports, such as David Beckham, are hardly living on the breadline.

We need more creativity, not less. We need more pupil engagement and enjoyment, not less. We need to be able to show children why their education is relevant and how it can help them with so much more than getting a 'good' job and earning lots of money. Especially at a time when graduates are not earning much more than their non-university-educated peers, but have massive debts to pay for the privilege.

The rate of change
in education

Imagine how tiring it must be to change the way you do your job several times a year. Someone in government with a particular agenda decides that schools should do something in a certain way and decrees that all schools must follow this advice and that they will be judged according to how this advice is implemented.

A couple of years later there is a new government and/ or a new education secretary, so the 'old ways' are debunked. All the work schools and teachers have done, all the time they have spent and all the resources they have purchased are now obsolete and they must start again with a completely different agenda.

Now imagine that happening with a dozen or more other initiatives being introduced as well during that time. The cost to taxpayers is enormous, and the energy of teachers is being sapped. But most worrying of all, the education of our country's children is being used as a political football: something to enhance the CVs of certain politicians rather than a system that ensures progress and opportunities for young people in education.

Even those working in education would struggle to name all the education secretaries we have had in the last decade (if only we could forget Gove). None seems to remain in post long enough for their personal vision to become a reality before another comes along and changes everything to suit their own educational Utopia. After a few years of this, anyone would become jaded. After several years, cynicism sets in. I would imagine that, after thirty years, one would finally realise that the ideals they had when they came into teaching are merely pipe dreams and will never happen, despite the amount of effort they put in. Their vocation becomes just that job they have to see through to the end with pension intact.

Stop politicians wrecking education

A decent, high quality education shouldn't be available only to those with money, yet this is the state of education in Britain today.

The top independent primary school in my locality uses elements of the key stage 3 curriculum with its key stage 2 pupils. I work privately with ten year olds who are doing the kinds of maths and English problems their state school counterparts won't touch until they are much older. I work with GCSE pupils from state schools who have not had the opportunity to learn many of the things the more fortunate (and often, but not exclusively, more affluent) fee-paying students are able to learn.

I don't agree that we should abolish independent schools: there really is no merit in dumbing everything down just to make things equal. What does need to be done is to make state schools more comparable with good independent schools, and the first thing that needs doing is to take all schools away from government control.

There has been quite a bit of political rhetoric about how state schools can learn from independent ones, but without extra funding and increased school autonomy, this is an impossible goal.

Currently, state schools are tied by government targets that have no positive (and often have a negative) influence on the education their pupils are likely to receive. Many of the

93

harmful aspects of modern education that government ministers force on state schools have been ditched by independent schools because they know the difference between rote learning and understanding. They place equal importance on sporting and artistic achievement as they do on academia, thus ensuring their pupils receive a more rounded educational experience.

Independent schools also have more control over the type of behaviour they expect their teachers to deal with. In state schools, there is a government bar on the number of pupils who can be excluded for poor behaviour. In their efforts to meet unrealistic targets, state schools are holding on to their sub-human pupils, but then they have the problem of classroom behaviour, which has a knock-on effect on attainment for other pupils.

One typical example came to my attention a couple of years ago. A secondary school in Northamptonshire, which had gone from special measures to outstanding in a very short time, was subsequently slated by Ofsted for excluding too many pupils, and had its outstanding status removed.

Surely it stands to reason that a school that doesn't tolerate unreasonable behaviour from its pupils stands more chance of providing an outstanding education. Just imagine it: a school where teachers can actually teach and where decent pupils can actually learn. It seems, however, that Ofsted wants it both ways: keep those pupils who have never been taught - or who simply refuse - to behave in a reasonably civilized manner, whilst also getting the best from every child.

This is a situation that rarely troubles the independent sector. Generally, classes are smaller, but it's the fact that parents are paying that ensures pupils work hard and teachers can be teachers rather than riot controllers. No parent paying thousands of pounds a term for their child's education will put up with another child disrupting that.

For this reason, an increasing number of not terribly affluent parents are paying more than they can afford just to ensure their children are able to go to a school that provides a decent education, rather than the sorry target-ridden and meaningless drivel that is becoming the staple of many state schools in certain areas. But parents shouldn't have to run up debts just to ensure that their children acquire the good education that is everyone's right. The state should be ensuring that every child, no matter what his or her background, has the same opportunities as a child in an independent school. Whether every parent and child appreciates and grasps that opportunity should be down to them, and schools should not have to bear the burden of those who do not value education. (I'd say there's a separate argument here, and one that should involve some kind of boarding school set-up for the children of such families, but that'll have to wait until I'm running education.)

As a teacher, I noticed that, without exception, the parents who made the loudest noise about unfair exclusions were the ones whose spawn delighted in disrupting lessons for the majority of pupils from decent families. If a poll had been conducted as to whether or not unruly pupils should be excluded, the majority of parents would have voted 'yes' - and so too would the majority of pupils. Yet we continue to pander to the 'cultural underclass': those who do not value education and think it's acceptable to ruin it for everyone else. All because we have to reach arbitrary government targets set by twats who have probably never met a state school pupil; who don't understand education but see it as an opportunity to become a hero of social history.

It's time for schools to run themselves. If the majority of parents and pupils agree with exclusions for certain types of behaviour, then that's exactly what the school should provide. They don't need do-gooders (whose own kids go to exclusive schools, even if those schools are disguised as 'ordinary' ones) telling them that they have to put up with vile behaviour. If any parent dislikes the school's policies, the school should be at liberty to tell them that they can take their little tosser elsewhere.

Some will argue that we would be left with a situation whereby certain kids won't be accepted by any school, but ultimately that would probably be a good thing. Only when parents are given full responsibility for the actions of their own children might they begin to act responsibly towards them. I can see no better way of ensuring that parents point their offspring in the right direction than by forcing them, for 24 hours a day, to put up with the devil spawn they've brought into the world, rather than letting it loose on the rest of the decent population.

At the moment, the bigger the arseholes, the more benefit they get from the current system, and that needs to change. And the biggest arseholes of all are the politicians allowing this to happen.

The only way to rescue education is to get politicians out of it.

Inclusion

It is fantastic that pupils who were once barred from a mainstream education can now have access to it if they and their parents wish. For so many children, mixing with others at school does much for their self-esteem and helps them realise that, despite any differences, they have a lot in common with other children and have the potential to live a full life. Schools now have wheelchair access, disabled toilets, special computers and other equipment to help those who have problems handling pens and pencils, assistants who can be used in dozens of ways to ensure that children previously denied a mainstream education and consigned to special schools can today enjoy the same benefits as other children.

Sounds perfect, doesn't it?

However, for all the positive elements that inclusion has brought, there are many negatives; some enough to destroy education for others.

For many children today, behaviour seems to be a concept far removed from anything witnessed in schools 20 or 30 years ago. This is such a huge problem that it has its own chapter; however, it is worth acknowledging here how the behaviour of some children with Special Educational Needs (**SEN**) can have an impact on classes all over Britain.

I am acquainted with many teachers who work in primary schools and, from what they tell me, it sounds as if they have a much harder time than secondary teachers. One young teacher has told me about Jason, a Year 6 student (aged 10-11) with special needs. He can just about write his name legibly -

although capital letters are alien to him - but try to get him to write anything else and apparently you'll be waiting a very long time.

All through primary school, Jason's teachers and the special educational needs co-ordinator (SENCo) have tried to get him a statement. A statement of special educational needs means that the school receives extra funding in order to employ an assistant to work with a pupil, ensuring that he/ she gets the help he/ she needs. Without this, the child is left to flounder unless the teacher directs most of her/ his time and attention on the pupil, which is what invariably happens when the child's behaviour becomes destructive. This means that others in the class miss out on the teacher's time and therefore do not reach their potential in lessons.

Why is it, then, that Jason does not have a statement? Because his parents do not want him to be tested. They have used their right to send Jason to a mainstream school (and to be honest, with government cuts there probably wouldn't be enough special school places anyway) but have reneged on their responsibilities by refusing to let his school go through the procedures needed to help Jason. They don't want their child to be treated differently, even though the teacher now has to focus all her attention on one child rather than the whole class. Apparently the school cannot (or will not) do anything about this.

And Jason isn't the only pupil in this situation. So many parents see primary school as a place they can drop off their children for a few hours of free childcare, with no appreciation of the educational element of school. They don't care either that their child's needs are preventing other children from getting the quality of teaching they deserve.

98

As for those who are statemented, they very often have to share their assistant with others who, like Jason, are not covered for extra funding.

Actually getting help for special needs in the primary sector is a real battle, and one example of this is in the next chapter. Even where parents do accept that their children need help – indeed, where parents beg for that help – there's a long fight ahead.

Unless a child is deemed by psychologists and other agencies to merit full time help (more on this farce in the next chapter) they are not issued with a statement, yet still the school will be issued with criteria to which they have to adhere in order to meet the child's needs; this comes without extra funding or resources of any kind. The majority of SEN pupils fall under this blanket, and teachers have to find ways of meeting their needs whilst seeing to those of the rest of the class. Throw in behaviour problems as well, and you have an impossible situation.

Not all SEN pupils have behavioural difficulties in the way we might think: some misbehave due to frustration and insecurity; some don't go out of their way to disrupt, but their self-esteem and other emotional needs are such that the teacher has to spend more time with them. And, of course, behaviour problems are not exclusive to those children with SEN.

Another primary teacher told me that one year 6 pupil he taught was barely able to write a sentence each lesson. Most of this was laziness - he'd just given up over the years. His mum understood the teacher's frustrations but said that she had decided not to push the child as this was making him miserable and more stubborn. She suggested that the teacher do the same.

The teacher in question was bloody tempted: that had been a particularly heavy year for special needs and he was stretched beyond the limit, as was his assigned TA. However, there was no way the school, the LEA, the governors or Ofsted would have let him get away with that. He had to show for every lesson that the boy had improved in some way academically, even when he refused to write a word.

There is a primary school local to me that, for a while, was one of the few in the county to have a designated SEN class for some of the more needy children: a 'nurture group' as it was called. It did a great job in easing troubled pupils into mainstream classes by working with small groups for a sustained period. However, the level of funding that went into those few pupils was disproportionate to the amount spent on all the children and was deemed unfair by many. Lack of funding soon put paid to that initiative, anyway, and before long those kids were struggling again in the classroom, as were their teachers and, more worryingly, their classmates.

Very often, inclusion for a few children means exclusion for the rest.

School data and the battle to help SEN pupils
Data and statistics play a big role in education today, and every teacher knows that the information on pupils that is passed from one academic year to the next needs to be taken with a large bucket of salt.

Transition from primary to secondary is no exception, and it is always interesting to hear from our primary teaching colleagues the 'true' stories behind the students coming into year seven.

Primary schools have to put up with a hell of a lot of patronising flak, particularly from outside agencies. As mentioned in the previous chapter, if a school asks for help with a struggling or 'behaviourally challenged' child, they are expected to jump through all kinds of hoops to 'prove' that the child needs extra support and cannot cope in a mainstream school.

As with too many parents, many involved with education seem to ignore primary schools' importance during the formative years of a child's engagement with education, and the rubbish that primary schools have to put up with is incredible. Children who would be sent to special schools or **PRUs** in their secondary years are entitled to be educated in mainstream primaries, despite the disruptions they cause, and their often dangerous behaviour.

Of course, it is then down to the secondary schools to do something about it, but by then the rot has set in.

I remember being livid about the data on a year seven boy who had, apparently, managed to achieve level 4s in his **KS2** tests but who could barely write his name when in my class without causing the most almighty fuss. I was expected to teach him English at a level way beyond his ability, but because the data said he was capable, I was expected to carry on regardless. His behaviour and emotional state were beyond the pale, and I could not believe that he had managed to get so far with no statement of educational needs, let alone managed to survive in a mainstream primary school.

101

At that time, I was the transition manager of our school, responsible for liaising with feeder primary schools. I contacted this boy's former year six teacher and she replied with the following (which she has given permission for me to include here):

Andrew joined our school as a Year 3, when I was the Year 3 teacher. It quickly became apparent to me and the teaching assistant that he was unteachable. I hate that word, but he really was.

We went through the myriad form-filling exercises and by the end of that year managed to get an educational psychologist to come and observe Andrew in class. By this time this one child had managed to disrupt a whole year's lessons for the other pupils.

The ed psych gave me a list of things I should be doing to support Andrew – things that would have meant my being unable to work with other children during lessons and making too many allowances for poor behaviour that would have an impact on the rest of the class.

When I explained this to the head, she told me that I had a negative attitude and would be wholly accountable for the child's lack of improvement if I did not follow the advice given.

Just to illustrate how useless some of this advice was, here is one example:
* *At the beginning of each lesson, issue the child with 10 paperclips.*
* *Make the child aware that this is how many times he can demand your attention*

- *Each time he demands your attention, you must see to his needs but then remove a paper clip.*

The following day I explained to Andrew and his mother how this would work.

Cue first lesson:
Andrew was given paper clips and reminded of what was going to happen. At the start of the lesson, while the class was seated on the carpet, Andrew pulled a paper clip into a point and stabbed the girl next to him on her arm.

I removed the paper clip and explained that Andrew had lost one of his attention clips. The girl was sent to school office as she was crying about the hole in her shirt and the blood (admittedly not much) on her arm. Andrew was beginning to enjoy himself.

I resumed the lesson but was interrupted by a boy who had just had a paper clip thrown at him. I took another paperclip from Andrew and explained that he had lost his second. Andrew laughed and threw all the paperclips at me. I picked up paper clips and against my better judgment gave him seven back.

He threw them at me again.

Quietly I asked the teaching assistant to get him out of room before I throttled him. Andrew made a fuss and it took a few minutes to persuade him to leave the room. The lesson was wrecked

That evening, Andrew's mother came to see me, demanding to know why I hadn't kept my side of the bargain.

103

When the ed psych returned (many weeks later) she was disappointed with my progress and complained to the head teacher. I was subjected to a series of lesson observations as my ability to teach was now in serious doubt.

A couple of years later, by which time I was teaching Year 6 and Andrew was a lot worse, I managed to persuade the school's SENCO (Special Educational Needs Co-ordinator) to get help. I was encouraged to learn that my lesson would be visited by a different ed psych.

My hopes were dashed, however, when the paperclip method was once again suggested.

Thus, Andrew went through primary school causing disruption for his classmates, his teachers and the school data system. He was not progressing at the rate dictated by national expectations, and the school was perceived to be at fault. By the time Andrew was doing his Key Stage 2 National Tests, he was entitled to one-to-one help completing the papers, and this, I guess, was how the school ensured he achieved the level 4 expected of him.

*

This boy lasted in our secondary school until the middle of Year 7, when he was finally diagnosed properly and offered a place at the local PRU.

His time at primary school had been, at best, a money-saving exercise, which in reality cost a lot more in educational terms than the money saved, for him and for his fellow classmates.

The refusal to deal with issues such as the above can have more far-reaching effects on other children than just the disruption to their learning: it can also affect how they perceive fairness, and life in general.

A few years ago I inherited a year seven in my tutor group who was completely off the scale. The first time he ever spoke to me was to inform me that he had 'anger management issues'. I knelt down so my face was level with his and replied, 'So do I.'

Funnily enough, he didn't seem to have any tantrums during form time. I wish the same could have been said for other parts of the school day.

This boy was removed from classrooms on a daily basis and counselled by well-meaning but incompetent pastoral staff. He lapped it up. And what's more, the other kids, many of whom had seen the results of this boy's behaviour since primary school, could see that he was getting away with much more than they ever could because he 'has issues with behavior'.

There was nothing medically wrong with this lad, and one meeting with his mother was enough to convince me that he had been allowed to do what the fuck he pleased for as long as he could remember.

A group of kids from my form came to see me one lunch time to complain that this boy, who had been his usual foul self during period one, had been removed from the lesson and taken off with a pastoral care assistant to 'make pancakes'. He then made a special journey back to the classroom at the end of the lesson to tell the others what a great morning he was having.

This resulted in a few others trying their luck during period two.

Kids aren't stupid. If they get the message that vile behavior results in rewards, why the hell shouldn't they get in on the act?

Bureaucracy is more important than pupils' education

As with all public services, schools are obsessed with saving money, providing data and creating targets. It's easy to forget their main function: to educate children.

*

As I'm settling my year 10 pupils to begin the first lesson, the attendance administrator bustles into my classroom, looking officious and waving a print-out in front of her.

'Why have you marked Armani as absent? She's here.'

'She wasn't in here at tutor time,' I answer calmly, resisting the urge to kick her in the crotch and telling her not to interrupt my lesson.

'Well, she was with the pastoral care team,' she huffs. 'She's still traumatised by Amy's sudden death.' (Amy was not a friend of Armani's: Amy was Amy Winehouse, the singer who'd died the previous July, and about whom Armani had never revealed the slightest interest until returning from the summer holiday.)

The attendance administrator continues, 'This is the third registration error you've made recently.'

'It's hardly my error if I didn't know she was with the pastoral care team,' I reply. 'Someone should have informed me so I could mark her in.'

'If you'd been here on time, she would have told you herself. There was no one in your classroom when she came to tell you,'

'I was here at 7.30 but was called to a last-minute meeting. I will mark her in now.'

'Oh there's no need now. I've done it! It's a good job there wasn't a fire!' And with that, she stomps out of my classroom.

I become aware of the Y10s, who are gawping and giving me their rapt attention, for a change.

'Who the fuck does she think she is?' pipes up Summer.

I should give Summer a warning for swearing, but instead I decide I will find an excuse during the lesson to reward her with a giant bar of Galaxy. She'll understand why.

*

I hear from many teachers about the effect of bureaucracy on their ability to teach and how they are at the mercy of those who never need to work in a classroom.

Here's just one example from Alan, a maths teacher:
At our school, we're expected to fill out a form every time a pupils needs removing from the class, and this form has to be hand-delivered to one of the school receptionists. It's an absolute nightmare.

Apart from the time it takes to complete the form, some of the information has to be searched for on the school network, which isn't always working, but incomplete forms are ignored as the office staff are too busy to look up the information.

One of the big rules teachers have to obey is the 'no reading emails' during lessons, which is understandable, but the office staff often send us emails at the last minute and get really arsey if we don't read or respond to them immediately - especially if it's a last-minute break duty or bus duty or something.

Of course, while we're looking up pupil data on our laptops, we have to freeze the image on the board so the pupils can't read the personal information we're looking up, but then we are accused of reading emails.

Another problem is getting the completed form to reception. Someone has to take the form, and you can't always guarantee it'll get to where it should, and often the kid who needs removing blocks the door so whoever is taking the form can't leave the classroom.

Then if we do succeed in getting the form to the right person, some pen-pusher will decide it's not important, or that one of the sections hasn't been completed to their satisfaction, so no action is forthcoming.

The office staff are very quick to seek me out while I'm trying to rush my lunch at the same time I'm setting up for the afternoon's lessons, insisting that talking through the latest data report is more important than making sure I don't pass out from hunger during afternoon lessons.

Taking flak from paper pushers comes with the territory in schools, unfortunately. Over my teaching career, I have worked in five different schools, and in each of these classroom staff were routinely used to cover admin staff who were off sick, on holiday or simply 'overworked'. It never ceases to amaze me how number crunching, data and admin tasks have taken priority over actual teaching.

The classroom staff to whom I refer are not teachers (although some of the tasks passed on to teachers, which should be undertaken by office staff, is a whole other issue for which there isn't room here) but they are funded in order to work with pupils who need help, so using them to answer phones or photocopy for a member of admin staff is, in my view, stealing from the kids who are entitled to help.

'We don't need no education targets (and don't get no funding)'

When I was a kid (1960s and 70s) we didn't have classroom assistants. Or Teaching Assistants. Or Learning Support Assistants. Or whatever the correct term is at the moment. It was a class full of kids and the teacher - even in primary. There might have been a general dogsbody who cleaned up the paint pots and sharpened pencils, and there may have been volunteer parents who came in to read with the 'slow readers', but that was it.

Of course, teaching then wasn't the jumping-through-hoops job it is now. As with all public services, education today is a political football and senseless government targets and manipulation of statistics are everything.

As well as this, walk into any school in most areas and you will find kids in every classroom who just would not have been a problem 30 or 40 years ago. 'Emotional and Behavioural' needs were largely catered for in special schools. Many of the problems kids we have now did not exist then (probably because diet was better, fast food and instant service was a thing of the future, TVs had only three channels of rubbish and computer games didn't exist). Any kid who was rude to the teacher got a slap, followed by another one at home if the parents found out.

I went to an ordinary primary school in a very ordinary area, but I don't recall any problem kids. Never did a kid throw a chair at a teacher or call her a fat slag. And certainly never did a parent come in and threaten to smack the fat slag.

Parents generally supported what schools were trying to do for their offspring and didn't spend all their time complaining that it was the school's job to parent the kids, as many do today.

When families came into the community from other countries, children and parents learned pretty damned quick that it was in their interests to learn the language if they were to get anywhere; there was no sympathetic, unqualified mum off the playground being paid peanuts to do the work for children who didn't understand. And no one made excuses for them – it was sink or swim. (I'm not saying that's how it should be – just that that's how it was.)

And of course there were no league tables or targets. Or Ofsted.

Funding for schools is woefully inadequate. Check out this link if you're curious to see how it works: https://consult.education.gov.uk/funding-policy-unit/high-needs-funding-reform/supporting_documents/Current_funding_system.pdf

Since 2013, schools are supposed to be able to claim somewhere in the region of £6000 per SEN pupil: https://www.hiphackney.org.uk/downloads/CDC_funding_b riefing_for_parents_FINAL.pdf

Of course, the definition of SEN pupil is pretty arbitrary and seems to depend more upon how loud the parents can shout and whether they are prepared to go to the press.

For every kid in our schools today who receives funded help, there are about six more who have come over from another country where English is not spoken; about a dozen who you would be forgiven for thinking had been brought up by wolves (although I think wolves make better parents than some of the chavs whose kids I've tried to teach) and about half a dozen who are just plain barking. And that's not to mention those who have genuine learning difficulties that prevent them from accessing the curriculum.

It stands to reason that it costs an awful lot more than £6000 to help these pupils, however little it costs for classroom assistants. It also means that an awful lot of classes where students need genuine academic help are left to flounder, and just about every secondary school I'm acquainted with has at least one student in almost every class who barely understands the language, yet is expected to get five grade Cs (level 4 or 5) at GCSE.

During my last year as a teacher, our school was given an arbitrary target to meet regarding GCSE grades. It bore no relevance to the fact that this was a deprived area with a lot of third generation benefit claimants, teenage parents, grandparents in their 30s, drug abuse and violent crime, even among primary pupils. Overall (and there were exceptions when I taught there, as I'm sure there are today) there were low expectations or value placed on getting an education. It is an area that has featured negatively in the press and on the national news because of the crime rate, and supermarkets won't deliver in the area. Yet our targets for 5 or more GCSEs were the same as schools in more salubrious areas where the pupils left primary school able to read and write to a high standard, mainly because they were supported at home.

113

Therefore, our school often came out as 'inadequate' and even 'failing'. The fact that we had a high proportion of kids from dysfunctional backgrounds who could barely write their own names was overlooked. The fact that every class was, at some point during every lesson, disturbed by at least three students who had never been taught that some thoughts should stay in their heads; it was inappropriate to play pocket billiards (or worse) at their desks; it was not acceptable to throw a tantrum because the teacher said they couldn't spend the lesson watching DVDs just because there was only a fortnight until the half term holiday; who didn't even know how to sit in a chair and listen for two minutes - never were these problems properly taken into account when targets were thrown at us.

And never was the hard work, care and dedication of the staff acknowledged. Is it any wonder so many teachers are angry and bitter?

Time for more light relief

Jane was a primary teacher until 2010; here she shares this amusing story about her NQT year (just seven years prior to quitting).

I had a class of mixed year 4 and 5 children in a tough school. The head teacher was giving me some feedback on a lesson he had just observed, and he kept referring to my less-able group as 'the craft group.'

Not wanting to show my ignorance, I didn't ask what the term meant but quickly adopted it, being careful to use it when I referred to each group in class and on my lesson plans.

When the head was next observing my lesson, I noticed that he was sitting at the back of the classroom with his head in his hands. I was gutted, as I could only assume that my lesson was so dreadful he couldn't bear to watch. After about five minutes, though, I noticed his shoulders shaking and realised he was helpless with laughter. In some ways, that was much worse.

Anyway, when all the kids had gone out to break, I asked defensively what was so funny.

'The craft group,' he said, between fits of laughing. 'It's a staff room acronym for "Can't Remember A Fucking Thing"!'

Are you training to be a teacher?

Here are a few things to think about as you begin your teaching adventure:

You will notice in every staff room a large proportion of moaners and whiners.
When I began teaching, these people were just a handful, but over the years that number has increased. Don't make the mistake I made. I assumed these people were old, lazy, useless, and just looking for something to whinge about. I quickly realised that they were, in fact, professionals in the field of teaching who had seen it all before. They recognised a pig with lipstick whenever someone from SLT or the DfE tried to convince us all that we were looking at a never-before-dreamed-of initiative that would raise educational standards for ever and ever.

Unless you attack your pupils with an axe or openly have sex with one of your students, you are likely to be offered a promotion quite early in your teaching career.
Don't make the mistake I - and many others -made when promoted early on.

Chances are you have not been offered this promotion because your teaching skills are superior to those of older and more experienced staff; you have been offered this promotion because of one of the following:
i)   You are cheaper than the current post holder

ii)   You are more malleable than the current or other potential post holders (they've seen it all before and know too much)

iii)   No other mug wants to do it

The holidays do not make up for the shitty job of teaching.

i)   Half terms will be spent catching up with routine stuff you are expected to do but don't have time for during term time, and titivating your classroom.

ii)   Christmas and Easter holidays will be spent marking mock exam papers/practice SATs papers, reading up on the latest government initiatives and the school policies that will change as a result, and updating your classroom displays. And looking for a better school to work in. (That last one rarely ends well.)

iii)   Summer holidays will be spent reading up on the latest changes to the curriculum and exams; updating timetables and displays; planning - although these plans will be useless by the end of the first week back;* organising your classroom; if you teach English, you will need to read all the books you will be teaching the following year and be aware of the characters, plot, themes, etc; labelling books; if you work in secondary, you will need to spend several days of the summer holiday congratulating/consoling pupils and their parents following GCSE results; if your school has a sixth form, you will need to be there the previous week for A level results. That means trying to sort out problems with colleges, universities, UCAS, students, parents, ...

iv)   You will rarely feel as if you've had a proper break and will want to headbutt the next person who says they envy teachers their long holidays.

You are likely to be expected to take kids on trips outside of school hours - even some residential ones.

i) Don't expect to get any sleep, and certainly don't expect to get any appreciation. Any you do get will then be a bonus.

ii) You won't be paid for this, and very often it will be during your hard-earned holiday.

iii) Do expect to get lots of complaints from parents who haven't bothered to bring their kids up properly but who want to sue you when one of them gets hurt disobeying basic rules.

If you really want to teach, consider the independent sector.

In the state sector, you will be: a data inputter; nurse; social worker; counsellor (to pupils and parents); parent substitute; mediator; riot controller; political football; object of political, media and public scorn; scapegoat for all society's problems; responsible for not letting kids have time off during term time; responsible for fining parents; police officer, even when you see kids out and about in your free time; public relations officer; mind reader; Satan; the only constant person in the lives of many of your pupils; scapegoat for those above you in the pecking order who need to shift the blame for their poor decisions; target setter; bullseye hitter; ... and all-round fucking miracle worker.

When it comes to actual teaching - you know, setting work, teaching it, helping kids understand, assessing their work, giving individual and appropriate feedback, remembering that these are children and not numbers to be crunched ... well ... actual teaching is way down the list of priorities.

At the time of writing, the teaching profession is haemorrhaging good teachers and fewer than one third remain

118

in teaching five years after qualifying. Furthermore, a half of teachers surveyed in 2016 say they are seriously considering leaving the so-called profession. Here's a link to just one of the many reports to that effect.

https://www.theguardian.com/education/2017/jul/08/almost-a-quarter-of-teachers-who-have-qualified-since-2011-have-left-profession

So much for the lure of twelve weeks' holiday per year (ha!) and a gold-plated pension (double ha!)

If you find that teaching is taking over your life to the exclusion of all else - that you have no time for friends, family, socialising, sleeping or any other things normal people do to relax and have fun - there is no shame in ditching it.

The more you do, the more that will become the expectation, and so the more you will be given to do.

Teachers need to stand together to protect themselves, but currently so many are still fighting each other to be top dog, creating even more impossible standards.

* NEVER complete tasks set for staff before the absolute deadline, especially when it comes to reports and other kinds of data input. I learned the hard way that meeting deadlines results in having to do the same thing more than once because the pen pusher who assigned the task hadn't thought it through. You'll think you're organised, but really you will have just made more work for yourself.

Where's that British stiff upper-lip?

Have you noticed that, whenever there's a tragic death on the news, there is an abundance of footage showing sobbing people laying flowers and hugging one another? And interviews with people who never met the deceased but have been selected to sum up the community's grief? When did all that start?

When I was at school, during the dark ages, I remember quite a few kids dying of one thing or another over the years. One was knocked down and killed by a car when we were six. Another drowned when we were eight. Then, during the course of one academic year at secondary school, we had a whole spate: one brain tumour, one leukaemia, one murder, one suicide and one joy rider.

The leukaemia death was particularly hard for me as it was a good friend I'd known since primary school. I remember attending the funeral with several classmates, then returning to school for maths and English in the afternoon. No one was interested in why we were visibly upset.

As for the murder, it made the national press, which meant our school was a magnet for reporters and police for quite some time, and rumours were flying round that the perpetrator was probably one of our peers, which was rather unsettling for a bunch of fifteen-year-olds. And it shames me to admit this, but yes, it was a bit of excitement. That's kids for you - they thrive on the gory and they love a bit of drama. Teachers understood this, as did parents, and visible outpourings of emotion were discouraged. Stiff upper lip, and all that.

As a teacher more than 30 years later, I have witnessed the outpourings of grief following the death of pupils within schools I have worked. I have tried to console those who are entitled to feel real pain - siblings and close friends; however, I do feel that there is way too much pandering to teenage mass hysteria. I've seen year eights, who had never heard of a particular year 11 boy before he was killed crashing his brother's motorcycle, absolutely inconsolable during my lessons and having to be taken to see the member of the pastoral care team assigned to help the children deal with their grief. I have had year 10 girls insisting they cannot attend my lesson for the third time that week and must be counselled by a member of the pastoral care team as a result of the sudden death of the year seven whom they'd never met and who had been at the school all of two weeks before her tragic asthma attack.

I understand that children feel grief, I really do, and I understand that it is possible to be upset about the death of someone you've never met. But there is a definite tendency in schools for the wall-to-wall hugging and weeping that would normally be associated with a mass shooting. When this type of behaviour occurs following the news of the death of Norma Numbskull's cat just before period three, it's all I can do not to bang their heads together and tell them to get a grip and stop looking for attention.

Perhaps others don't feel like this. Perhaps this is further proof that I'm nothing but a bitter old git. Perhaps if I'd received a bit more sympathy after watching my childhood friend being put six feet under at the age of fifteen, I'd be a more compassionate and patient person now. But I do find it sickening when a bunch of kids - those same kids who can shrug off footage of small children around the world working in sweatshops to provide their trendy designer clothes - try to use the death of someone they neither knew nor cared about to get out of a maths lesson.

And even more sickening is the band of simpering adults allowing them to behave like this.

More light relief needed

Here's another amusing anecdote from Karen, this time recounting a theatre group's visit to the school.

Our head had organised a series of visiting theatre productions and all had been of a pantomime format, whereby the kids could participate and shout out as much as they liked.

Being a church school, though, we felt we should have something with a religious slant, so the head organised a small, two-person theatre performance about the life of Jesus.

The children sat through the first few minutes expectantly, eager to please the actors with their knowledge of how these things worked. After a while, however, they became fidgety and slightly confused: it was clear that the bloke was playing the same character- some dude called Jesus - but the woman kept changing her character, and the kids couldn't keep up.

They began to get a little more animated, though, when it came to the scene where Jesus is fasting in the desert. The female actor, wearing horns, a tail and carrying a trident, crept up behind Jesus.

'Behind you!' came a cheery shout from the back of the hall, to which the rest of the school excitedly joined in. 'Behind you! Behind you!'

Now, this was more like it. The kids sat up straighter and looked a lot happier. The actors, to give them credit, quickly recovered their professionalism.

'I can give you all these lands if you follow me,' said Satan.

'Oh no you can't ...' began Jesus, but he was cut off by a shout from the back. 'Oh yes she can!' (They weren't fooled by the male disguise, you see: canny kids, these.)

Others began chanting 'Oh yes she can!' but were disappointed that there was no subsequent volley of chants as to whether she could or couldn't.

Confusion was written across their little faces, and soon the children were once again happily conversing amongst themselves.

Then the scene requiring Jesus to carry the cross came up. The actor did an admirable job of pretending to be struggling, grunting and sweating, carrying the heavy cross that was obviously made of cardboard. But for some reason, the kids thought this was a long-awaited dash of comedy. They laughed and laughed.

Although embarrassed, I felt a strong urge to laugh too and decided to escort two hysterical year fours from the hall, one of whom was rolling on the floor holding her sides and the other who was laughing so much she was crying and choking. I spent the remainder of the performance with them in the corridor, too ashamed to go back in.

I arrived back just in time for the questions at the end. My heart sank when the actor pointed at one particular year five boy, who was not known for his common sense.

'Was this based on a true story?' the boy piped up.

124

I'm afraid that, at this point, I had to leave the hall rather quickly, as did several other members of staff who had also remembered something urgent they needed to do in their classrooms.

For the rest of my life, I will remember the scene from the staff room window that evening: two bemused actors loading up their van, getting in and taking one last look at the school sign before speeding off. They must have been checking it really was a 'church school' - and who can blame them?

And not many members of staff remained in assembly the following morning as the head tore a strip off the poor little buggers, who had no idea what they'd done wrong.

Meeting former pupils

I'm often privileged to meet former pupis and hear from them how they are getting on in the adult world.

Some take the trouble to thank me and to share specific things they remember from my lessons that have proved useful in their lives since leaving school. Some reminisce about our shared moments in detention, or the time I swore when Darren Dickhead dropped his bag on my foot. Some even apologise for being little arseholes, as they now appreciate that I was trying to help them.

Such reunions are not always so positive, though. One of my former colleagues (a maths teacher) was recently accosted in town by the mother of one of the most poorly behaved kids we'd ever taught. This mother was at pains to point out, rather aggressively, how well her son was doing now and how he'd never needed any of the stuff he'd been made to do in that teacher's lessons. She went on at great length, detailing how her son was now working in finance, living in London and earning more than this teacher could ever dream of, despite not turning up for one of his maths GCSE exams and failing spectacularly.

My mate was pissed off. He'd just been enduring a day of shopping with his wife and daughter, trying to make the best of it. The last thing he needed was this harridan bellowing at him during the interminable wait outside New Look's changing rooms.

I was amused when he shared this anecdote, though, because a few months before, another former colleague from that school had told me that this same boy wiped down the table beside hers whilst she was visiting a nearby service station cafe. He'd asked her what he would need to do in order to retake his exams: he hated his job and couldn't afford to leave home, where his mum kept going on about what a little twat he was.

I happen to know that this young man is now receiving free private tuition, arranged by the ex-teacher his mother once threatened to take to court for infringing her son's human rights. (The teacher gave him a detention for not doing his homework.)

It seems that, for some - and not necessarily just the pupils - no matter how much we try to help kids, teachers will always be the enemy.

If I were Education Secretary

I can't possibly do so much ranting without offering a few solutions, so for what it's worth, here's how I would try to improve things:

- Take all admin tasks away from teachers: their skills are too precious to be wasted on such crap. If there were enough funds (which there aren't) I'd insist that every teacher was allocated a PA. As it stands, every department should have its own secretary – someone who is literate and won't make stupid errors on letters going out to parents (which, unfortunately, rules out a number of school admin staff I've come across in the last few years).

- Make all parents, pupils and teachers sign a school contract. Such contracts do already exist but are not worth the paper they're written on. If, for example, a parent sends their child to a school with a strict uniform policy, they will be responsible for ensuring their child abides by that policy. If they don't, they can take their child to a school with a policy that suits them better rather than resorting to blackmail by going to the press when their daughter is told to wear a skirt (or trousers) that don't show off her knickers.

- If a child is a little shit, the school is at liberty to expel it and the parent is responsible for teaching it some manners before sending it back. If the parent continues to allow the foul behaviour, the child will be sent to a state-funded boarding school with specialist teachers who can teach it something during term time (and possibly get some of their learning to rub off on their feckless parents during school holidays).

- All schools will ensure they are set up for children, parents and staff with disabilities, and funding will be available for this. (The funding will be taken from the current practice of

128

providing one-to-one teaching for kids who are just little arseholes with arsehole parents.)

- Children with SEN can attend mainstream schools as long as their behaviour and needs don't disrupt the learning of their classmates. If their behaviour is an issue, they will attend a school where staff are specially trained to deal with their needs.

- The curriculum will be widened to ensure that all talents are catered for and that every child is able to excel in at least one of their subjects.

- School reports will be set out so that each child's best subjects are at the front and take up the most space, unlike the current practice – particularly in primary schools - of giving priority to maths and English and one sentence (if that) to other subjects such as music, art, games, cookery, drama and IT.

- League tables will be abolished: there is no place for competition – where there have to be losers as well as winners – in education.

- Pupils will be accountable for their input into their own learning: scrotes who don't put in the work will not be given a leg-up by already hard-working teachers.

- Teachers will not be assessed on their ability to teach to the test and will not be accountable for every arsehole who refuses to work.

- Targets for progress will be based on the skills children need to work on to reach that next step of their development and not compared with school or national averages. Each child progresses at a different rate and needs to see personal progress rather than how they compare with others.

- All compulsory formal tests at primary school will be abolished and assessments will be conducted by the people who know the children's abilities: their teachers. These assessments will be of a format that suits the child. Some love

129

tests and thrive on them, but others panic and underperform. Let them undertake formal tests if that's what they want, but don't make those who can only fail go through that torture at such a young age.

• Pupils of all ages will experience practical lessons as well as theoretical ones, especially those primary children currently deprived of science and geography, subjects that require practical experiences and observations.

• Secondary school assessments will change to reflect the world we live and work in. Coursework will be reintroduced so that the real skills needed in life and work are practised, alongside some of the more formal exams for subjects such as maths.

• Only qualified teachers or highly qualified individuals will teach classes, and they will teach only those subjects for which they are qualified or can prove knowledge well beyond that required by their pupils.

• All teachers will be paid according to their experience and dedication – not arbitrary targets and random results.

• Teachers with a higher workload will be paid more. For example, maths and English are compulsory throughout school, so the teachers of these subjects are significantly busier than those who teach subjects such as history or design technology that are optional after year nine. What's more, the marking load for English teachers far exceeds that of any other subject, so they should be accorded more free periods in which to complete good quality assessment.

• School librarians will be given the same status as teachers: they are just as important, if not more so.

• Only experienced teachers will be given leadership roles in schools, and will continue with some regular teaching commitments so they don't lose touch with the reality of the classroom. This goes for head teachers as well.

- Only experienced teaching professionals will interview teachers. Kids will not.
- Education will be for learning, not for political point scoring.
- Schools will be for pupils, and set up to help teachers teach. Admin staff will be there to take on those admin roles that support teaching and that teachers should not have to do. Admin staff will not have the power or authority to tell teachers how to do their jobs.
- Governors will be trained to a higher standard than they are now and paid accordingly. They will show that they are there to help the school succeed, not for their own personal agenda.

I'll stop there, but be assured that I have many more ideas. I may also change my mind, so ask me again next week.

What would you do to improve education?
Let me know.

angryexteacher.wordpress.com

Twitter: @angryexteacher

Facebook: https://www.facebook.com/Angry-Ex-Teacher-1216442031721674/?fref=ts

GLOSSARY

Just in case you are a new teacher or left the profession more than a decade ago …

Capability Proceedings: A procedure whereby a member of school staff is presented with concerns about their performance and subjected to an intense observation schedule. Meant for dealing with sub-standard staff, but increasingly used by corrupt, self-serving head teachers to intimidate teaching staff who they see as a threat to their power.

Controlled Assessments: These replaced GCSE coursework in 2010. Pupils had a set amount of time to complete a task that would go towards their final GCSE mark. These tasks had to be completed under teacher supervision in the classroom and under exam conditions. Apart from being a waste of teaching time, they didn't work – for many reasons.

HLTA: Higher Level Teaching Assistant. A teaching assistant who has been trained to a level close to that of a new teacher, but with a fraction of the salary. Often used to save money meant for qualified teachers.

In Loco Parentis: Latin for 'in place of parents'. Teachers are responsible for children in school and out when parents are not around.

KS2: What used to be called 'juniors'. Primary-school children aged seven to eleven who are in years three to six.

LEA: Local Education Authority. Traditionally in charge of local schools, but being squeezed out by the academy and free school agendas. Now have less power over schools but still responsible for the aspects politicians don't want to deal with.

Literacy Co-ordinator/ Leader: Teacher responsible for whole school organisation of English teaching and staff training.

Maths Co-ordinator/ Leader: Teacher responsible for whole-school organisation of maths teaching and staff training.

Mini-plenary: Plenaries are for the end of each lesson, a procedure used to assess how well pupils have learned that day's lesson objective. A mini-plenary is used within the lesson to gauge a running assessment of what the class has learned so far. Or not.

NQT: Newly Qualified Teacher. Usually a teacher who is in the first year of teaching following teacher training.

Ofsted: Office for Standards in Education. Replaced Her Majesty's Inspectors (HMI) in 1992. A well-meaning organisation set up to ensure school standards remained high, but which has disappeared up its own arse over the years and can't decide what it's for. Also used to bully nursery schools and child minders into making small children meet academic targets against the wishes of many parents.

PRUs: Pupil Referral Units. Institutions geared up to work with pupils who cannot cope in mainstream schools, usually because of behaviour issues.

Report Cards: Issued to kids who need reminding of normal values. They contain targets for the kids to meet, such as

134

'Don't throw things at your classmates' and 'Don't tell your teacher to fuck off'.

SATs: Statutory Assessment Tests. These are taken usually at age seven and age eleven in primary schools, but there are versions for secondary pupils as well. They are largely meaningless and don't have a great reputation.

SLT: Senior Leadership Team. Responsible for school decisions and performance. Usually includes the head/ principal, deputy head/ deputy principals, assistant heads/ assistant principals, and other higher-ranking staff.

TA: Teaching Assistant. Someone who is paid peanuts to help out in the classroom by working with individuals or small groups of children. Currently used to replace the dwindling number of qualified teachers. The quality of TAs is variable according to the school, but many have degrees and even teaching qualifications.

SEN: Special Educational Needs. These can be anything from behaviour and emotional issues to physical obstacles to mainstream learning.

SENCo: The member of staff responsible for ensuring children with SEN are catered for appropriately. This is traditionally a post requiring specialist training and skills.

Statement/ Statemented: A Statement of Special Educational Needs is a formality that marks out a pupil as needing extra funded help in school. Getting a child statemented means acquiring a statement, something that is notoriously difficult to achieve.

135

TES: Times Educational Supplement. A weekly newspaper focusing on educational matters. Its website includes a community forum for teachers.

Year 11 Prom: Imported from America. An evening during which school leavers celebrate the end of their formal education by getting rat-arsed, having guilt-tripped their parents into spending an extortionate amount of money on dresses, tuxedos and limos.

Printed in Poland
by Amazon Fulfillment
Poland Sp. z o.o., Wrocław

50926468R00081